TIMOTHY TITUS *and* HEBREWS

Published by
The Bible Reading Fellowship
15 The Chambers, Vineyard
Abingdon, OX14 3FE
United Kingdom
Tel: + 44 (0)1865 319700
Email: enquiries@brf.org.uk
Website: www.brf.org.uk
ISBN 978 1 84101 119 6

First published 2001
10 9 8 7 6 5 4 3 2 1
Reprinted 2008

Acknowledgments
Unless otherwise stated, scripture quotations are taken from The New Revised Standard Version of the Bible, copyright © 1989, 1995 by the Division of Christian Education of the National Council of the Churches of Christ in the United States of America, and are used by permission. All rights reserved.

New English Bible copyright © 1961, 1970 by Oxford University Press and Cambridge University Press

Extracts from The Book of Common Prayer 1662, the rights of which are vested in the Crown in perpetuity within the United Kingdom, are reproduced by permission of Cambridge University Press, Her Majesty's Printers.

p. 203 Extract by Sydney Carter copyright © 1971 Stainer & Bell Ltd, London, England

A catalogue record for this book is
available from the British Library

Printed in Singapore by Craft Print International Ltd

Timothy Titus *and* Hebrews

The People's Bible Commentary

Dick France

A Bible Commentary for Every Day

Introducing the People's Bible Commentary series

Congratulations! You are embarking on a voyage of discovery—or rediscovery. You may feel you know the Bible very well; you may never have turned its pages before. You may be looking for a fresh way of approaching daily Bible study; you may be searching for useful insights to share in a study group or from a pulpit.

The People's Bible Commentary (PBC) series is designed for all those who want to study the scriptures in a way that will warm the heart as well as instructing the mind. To help you, the series distils the best of scholarly insights into the straightforward language and devotional emphasis of Bible reading notes. Explanation of background material, and discussion of the original Greek and Hebrew, will always aim to be brief.

- If you have never really studied the Bible before, the series offers a serious yet accessible way in.
- If you help to lead a church study group, or are otherwise involved in regular preaching and teaching, you can find invaluable 'snapshots' of a Bible passage through the PBC approach.
- If you are a church worker or minister, burned out on the Bible, this series could help you recover the wonder of scripture.

Using a People's Bible Commentary

The series is designed for use alongside any version of the Bible. You may have your own favourite translation, but you might like to consider trying a different one in order to gain fresh perspectives on familiar passages.

Many Bible translations come in a range of editions, including study and reference editions that have concordances, various kinds of special index, maps and marginal notes. These can all prove helpful in studying the relevant passage. The Notes section at the back of each PBC volume provides space for you to write personal reflections, points to follow up, questions and comments.

Each People's Bible Commentary can be used on a daily basis, instead of Bible reading notes. Alternatively, it can be read straight through, or used as a resource book for insight into particular verses of the biblical book.

If you have enjoyed using this commentary and would like to progress further in Bible study, you will find details of other volumes in the series listed at the back, together with information about a special offer from BRF.

While it is important to deepen understanding of a given passage, this series always aims to engage both heart and mind in the study of the Bible. The scriptures point to our Lord himself and our task is to use them to build our relationship with him. When we read, let us do so prayerfully, slowly, reverently, expecting him to speak to our hearts.

CONTENTS

	Introduction	11
1	Paul, Timothy and Titus	18
2	What has it got to do with us?	20
3	A daunting task	22
4	Law and gospel	24
5	Paul's testimony	26
6	Fight the good fight	28
7	Prayer comes first	30
8	Men and women at prayer	32
9	The silencing of women	34
10	Qualifications for church leadership	36
11	More about leadership	38
12	The mystery of our religion	40
13	Dangerous delusions	42
14	Spiritual fitness	44
15	Look after yourself	46
16	Care for widows	48
17	More about widows	50
18	Church elders	52
19	Various instructions	54
20	Godliness with contentment	56
21	Taking it seriously	58
22	Final instructions	60
23	Timothy's faith and gift	62
24	Suffering for the gospel	64
25	Deserters and a good friend	66
26	No gains without pains	68
27	Faithfulness—ours and God's	70
28	The power of a word	72
29	The Lord's servant	74
30	Testing times	76
31	The marks of an apostle	78
32	The value of scripture	80

33	A solemn charge	82
34	'I have finished the race'	84
35	Personal messages	86
36	Paul on trial	88
37	'The faith we share'	90
38	Blameless 'bishops'	92
39	Portrait of the opposition	94
40	Duties of various groups	96
41	God's special people	98
42	New life in Christ	100
43	Final instructions	102
44	An odd sort of letter?	104
45	Who wrote Hebrews?	106
46	Who were 'the Hebrews'?	108
47	What is Hebrews all about?	110
48	Making sense of Hebrews	112
49	God's last word	114
50	Above the angels	116
51	The supremacy of the Son	118
52	Beware of 'drifting'!	120
53	Lower than the angels	122
54	Jesus, our elder brother	124
55	The perfect saviour	126
56	The servant and the Son	128
57	The importance of 'today'	130
58	Failure in the wilderness	132
59	God's rest—and ours	134
60	The sword of God	136
61	Christian confidence	138
62	Qualifications for priesthood	140
63	Perfect through suffering	142
64	Time to grow up	144
65	The danger of apostasy	146
66	After the stick, the carrot	148
67	The anchor of the soul	150

68 Enter Melchizedek 152
69 Greater than Abraham 154
70 A new type of priesthood 156
71 A priest for ever 158
72 Perfect for ever 160
73 The heavenly sanctuary 162
74 A new covenant 164
75 Lessons from the old sanctuary 166
76 Worshipping the living God 168
77 Why Christ died 170
78 Once for all 172
79 'I have come to do your will' 174
80 A single sacrifice for sins 176
81 Making the most of it 178
82 Another solemn warning 180
83 Living by faith 182
84 Seeing the invisible 184
85 Noah and Abraham 186
86 Seeking a homeland 188
87 More about the patriarchs 190
88 From Egypt to the promised land 192
89 Still looking forward 194
90 Racing to the finish 196
91 A positive view of suffering 198
92 Parental discipline 200
93 Pressing on 202
94 A tale of two mountains 204
95 One last warning 206
96 Angels unawares 208
97 Trusting God 210
98 Outside the camp 212
99 Final instructions 214
100 Signing off 216

PBC Timothy, Titus & Hebrews: Introduction

These four books of the New Testament are here grouped in one volume for publishing convenience, rather than because they naturally belong together: 1 and 2 Timothy and Titus form a natural group, but Hebrews is in a quite different category. We shall therefore deal with introductory matters at the beginning of the study of each book individually, but before we do so it may be helpful to take up a couple of more general questions which affect them all in different ways.

Letters of Paul?

In the Authorized Version, all four of the letters we shall be studying in this volume are described as 'Epistles of Paul the Apostle'. But many scholars today do not believe that Paul wrote any of them. It will be useful to find out why, before we look at the letters themselves.

1 and 2 Timothy and Titus

The first three letters are closely related together, and are generally described as a group as the 'Pastoral Epistles', because they are letters written by a pastor (church leader) to a pastor. Unlike most of the letters of Paul, each of them is written not to a church community but to an individual: Timothy and Titus appear in the letters as Paul's 'deputies' appointed to look after the church respectively in Ephesus and in Crete. All three letters begin with greetings from 'Paul, an apostle of Jesus Christ', and all consist of instructions from the apostle to his trusted associate, together with some quite personal information and comment (see especially 2 Timothy 4:9–22). They read like genuine letters, dealing with a specific local situation.

Why then does anyone doubt that Paul wrote them? Here are some reasons:

- The language and style are different from those of Paul's other letters.
- They seem to reflect a later situation in the church, when structures and officers have become more formal.

- The theology expressed has a different 'feel' from other letters of Paul, and is thought to reflect a later stage of Christian thinking, more settled and less urgent.
- It is not possible to fit these letters, and the situation they presuppose, into the life of Paul as we know it from Acts (which finishes with Paul in prison in Rome in AD62), and we have no clear information about what happened to him after that.

The last point is an argument from silence, and it is not difficult to construct a scenario following on from the end of Acts into which these letters would fit, even though such a reconstruction must remain speculative. It would suppose that Paul was released from prison, resumed his travels in the Eastern Mediterranean (including Ephesus and Crete), taking Timothy and Titus with him and leaving them to look after the churches in those areas, and was then re-arrested, tried (twice, 2 Timothy 4:16) and executed, as tradition has always maintained, along with Peter in Rome under Nero in about AD65.

The other arguments are more subjective, and some scholars are more impressed by the similarities with the other letters of Paul than the differences. Letters to a church leader to guide him on local pastoral and organizational problems are bound to 'feel' different from letters written to whole church communities. All Paul's letters focus on particular issues, and these are bound to vary from church to church. We cannot expect him to say the same things in all of them. Moreover, by AD65 it would be ten years since Paul wrote his longer letters, and at least three years since his other letters from prison; in that time both the situation and his thinking are bound to have moved on, and we could hardly expect him to sound quite the same.

The differences in language and style offer what seems a more objective argument, but the issue is clouded by the fact that Paul seems to have used a secretary to write most of his letters, and secretaries vary! We do not know how much freedom Paul allowed to people like Tertius, who 'wrote' Romans (Romans 16:22). Clearly he would read and approve what had been written before endorsing it in his own hand (1 Corinthians 16:21; Galatians 6:11; Colossians 4:18; 2 Thessalonians 3:17), but it is likely that the style of writing would depend a lot on the secretary. It is possible that in these three letters, with their more personal tone and with no indication of a secretary being involved, we are actually closer to the real language of Paul himself than in many of the other letters which he signed.

Some writings from the ancient world are clearly 'pseudonymous'—that is, written in the name of someone other than the actual author—and were apparently readily recognized as such. Usually their supposed authors were famous people of long ago, such as Enoch, Moses or Elijah, and few readers would have thought that those worthies actually wrote them. The use of such a famous name was perhaps a way to claim a greater authority for the work than the actual author could wield, and sometimes perhaps a way of expressing appreciation for their teaching or example by claiming to stand in their tradition.

But for someone to write 'in the name of' Paul so soon after his lifetime is a rather different enterprise, especially when we observe that these three letters are so personal and so closely fitted to specific local problems. Of course someone writing 'in Paul's name' could do that, but it is not easy to explain why someone writing to uphold Christian standards of truth and to oppose deceit would go to such lengths to make them sound authentic when they were not. The details would have to be carefully researched, and the author would have to have no qualms not only about using Paul's name, but even about 'impersonating' his quite intimate thoughts and needs in prison. And there is evidence that early Christians did not take kindly to people who, with the best of motives, invented stories about the apostles. At least one such in the second century was dismissed from the office of presbyter when his 'forgery' was discovered, even though he claimed to have done it 'out of love for Paul'!

In this commentary I shall take the letters at their face value, and refer to their author as simply 'Paul'. They claim to be the words of Paul to Timothy and Titus, and we shall read them as such. If you remain sceptical about their authorship, as many do, I hope that will not stop you appreciating and finding food for thought in what they have to say.

Hebrews

With Hebrews, the situation is quite different. Hebrews does not name its author (the heading in the Authorized Version is not part of the Greek text), and has only the most minimal personal greeting at the end. Nothing in the letter indicates that it was written by Paul, unless it be the news about Timothy in 13:23—but who is to say that Timothy (if it is the same Timothy) never worked with anyone else except Paul, particularly if Hebrews was written after Paul's death? Its style and contents are quite unlike anything in Paul's letters, and suggest an author familiar with Alexandrian Jewish thought, which was not Paul's background. There is nothing here of the 'Pauline' character of the letters to Timothy and Titus. It does not claim any connection with Paul, and anyone wishing to pass it off as his work would have had to do a much better job than this!

Why, then, did anyone ever think it was by Paul? Paul was the great Christian letter-writer of the first century, and no other first-century letters were preserved anonymously, so it was perhaps natural to tidy up the situation by attaching it to Paul's letters. Besides, the letter's anonymity became a problem when the Church began to insist on apostolic authorship as a basis for accepting a writing as part of the sacred canon of the New Testament: how can you confidently claim the apostolic origin of an anonymous letter? So from quite an early date this letter was generally attached to the collection of Paul's letters, even though many who wrote about it in the first few centuries did not think it was actually by Paul, and various guesses were offered as to who wrote it. We shall mention some of these when we come to Hebrews later in this volume.

So there really is no basis for linking this anonymous letter with Paul, and we do it a disservice if we fail to treat it as a quite distinctive letter, making its own unique contribution to what we know about early Christian thought. Modern scholars often speak of its author as one of the great theologians of the first-century Church on a par with, but quite different from, that other great theologian, Paul. We do not know who he or she was, and in the commentary I will simply speak of him/her as 'the author'. And since to write 'he/she' all the time would be tedious, I shall refer to the author as 'he', as most (but not all) of those who have been proposed as the author were men.

Bishops, priests and deacons

While there is no historical connection between the Pastoral Letters and Hebrews, both writings, in quite different ways, raise issues relating to Christian leadership in the first century, and it may help if I offer a few general comments on the terms they use before we look at them separately.

Roman Catholics and Anglicans have bishops, priests and deacons, and all these terms are used in these letters ('bishop' and 'deacon' in the Pastorals, 'priest' in Hebrews). Other churches have other titles for their ministers, particularly 'elder' ('presbyter'), and this term too occurs in the Pastorals. Paul's instructions to Timothy and Titus include significant sections on the selection and treatment of these ministers. So here we may expect to find useful New Testament perspectives on Christian ministry and leadership. What we find, however, may not be what our own use of these terms might lead us to expect.

'Bishops' (the Greek word might also be translated 'overseers' or 'superintendents') and 'elders' are apparently different names for the same people. They feature always as a group within a given church; there is no single 'bishop' or 'elder' who holds office on his own. If anyone in the Pastoral Letters is in such a position, it is Timothy and Titus, who are individuals brought in from outside to act under Paul's authority in their respective churches. But they are not called bishops; rather, the 'bishops' are those they appoint and oversee within the church, and these bishops (elders) are local people from within the church, not 'imports' like Timothy and Titus.

'Deacons' are a second tier, again spoken of as a group, and also consisting of local people. Their name ('deacon' means 'server') suggests that their function was more practical, perhaps along the lines first explored in Acts 6:1–6.

We shall think about what it meant to be a bishop or deacon when we come to 1 Timothy 3:1–13 and Titus 1:5–9.

But where are the 'priests'? In the Pastorals the word never occurs. In Hebrews it comes into its own, but in only two ways. It refers first to the priests of the Old Testament, whose role was to offer sacrifice in the tabernacle. But Hebrews argues that that role is now finished, and there is no more place for animal sacrifice or for the priests who offer it. In place of that corporate priesthood under the old covenant, we have not a new set of priests, but one great High Priest, Jesus the

Son of God, himself both priest and sacrifice in the new sanctuary which has replaced the old. His priesthood is exercised now in heaven, where he has gone after offering his one perfect sacrifice and where he now prays for his people on earth.

So there was an old corporate priesthood, which is now obsolete, and there is now instead a single High Priest in heaven. But in this letter, which speaks more of priesthood than any other part of the New Testament, there is no trace of a continuing priesthood on earth. Indeed the only mention in Hebrews of any office in the Church is a passing reference to 'your leaders' in chapter 13, with no more specific title. Where the idea of a Christian priesthood does occur in the New Testament (in 1 Peter 2:5, 9 and Revelation 1:6; 5:10; 20:6) it refers not to a group of people set apart for special ministry within the Church, but to the whole people of God, considered as a corporate 'priesthood'. But that idea is not taken up in Hebrews, for whom all legitimate priesthood is now focused in the one person of Jesus, the High Priest.

In the century after the New Testament was written, people began to make a distinction between 'bishop' and 'elder', with a single person being known as the 'bishop' (overseer) of the church in a given area, with a role of leadership over the 'elders'. The Greek word for 'elder' is *presbyteros*, and our English word 'priest' is derived from that word (even though it is not the word which is translated by 'priest' in the New Testament). So as time went on, a threefold pattern of bishop, priest and deacon became standardized.

As we approach these letters, we must be careful not to import our own understanding of these 'ministry' words back into them. We must recognize that both the words we use, and the nature of the offices they denote, have been through a long process of development. We are looking in these letters at churches in the early stages of developing a structure of leadership and authority, and we must read them with a due awareness of the distance between those early days and the structures we find in most churches today.

Suggestions for further reading

Gordon D. Fee, *1 and 2 Timothy, Titus* (New International Biblical Commentary, Hendrickson, 1984).

J.N.D. Kelly, *A Commentary on the Pastoral Epistles* (Black's New Testament Commentaries, A&C Black, 1963).

John Stott, *The Message of 2 Timothy* (The Bible Speaks Today, IVP, 1973).

Raymond Brown, *The Message of Hebrews* (The Bible Speaks Today, IVP, 1982).

F.F. Bruce, *The Epistle to the Hebrews* (New International Commentary on the New Testament, Eerdmans, 1990).

Donald Guthrie, *Hebrews* (Tyndale New Testament Commentaries, IVP, 1983).

Hugh W. Montefiore, *A Commentary on the Epistle to the Hebrews* (Black's New Testament Commentaries, A&C Black, 1964).

R.McL. Wilson, *Hebrews* (The New Century Bible, Marshall Morgan & Scott, 1987).

PAUL, TIMOTHY & TITUS

In the Introduction, I have explained why some people think Paul did not write these letters, and why I think it more likely that he did. Before we start reading them, it will be useful to fill out the brief sketch which I gave in the Introduction of the historical situation that they address.

Ephesus

Ephesus was the capital of the Roman province of Asia, a proud and magnificent city, which boasted among its great civic buildings one of the seven wonders of the ancient world, the gigantic Temple of Artemis. This great structure dominated the city. Its worship, which probably owed its popularity as much to its sexual activity as to any spiritual quality, was at the heart of civic life.

Paul spent more time in Ephesus than in any other of the churches he founded. You can read Luke's account of Paul's two or three years of missionary work in Ephesus in Acts 18:20—20:1, and his charge to the leaders of this young Christian church in Acts 20:17–38. He did not manage to go back there before his imprisonment in Rome, but if he was released after his first imprisonment (see Introduction) he would certainly have wanted to go back to this strategic centre, where he had spent so much time and suffered so much, and which was the key to the Christian mission in the western part of Asia Minor. It is a measure of its importance that he left Timothy to look after the church there, for Timothy was one of his most trusted associates.

But we shall see from the two letters that Timothy's task was not easy. He was a young man (1 Timothy 4:12)—Paul had known his grandmother (2 Timothy 1:5)! Not everyone in the church recognized his authority, and there were strong currents of teaching around among the Ephesian Christians which threatened the integrity of the Christian gospel. It was to confront such false teaching that Paul had left Timothy there (1 Timothy 1:3). The standards of behaviour among the local believers, living under the shadow of the Artemis cult, also left much to be desired. A firm hand was needed on the tiller, and Paul seems not to have been entirely sure that

Timothy had the leadership quality that was needed—indeed Timothy too seems to have had his doubts.

So the letters to Timothy try to strengthen his arm, and to remind him of how much is at stake. In the first letter, Paul hopes soon to be able to come and relieve Timothy (3:14–15; 4:13), but in the second letter the tone becomes more urgent, because Paul is now again in prison, facing the prospect of death, and the weight of responsibility will fall the more heavily on Timothy's shoulders. The future of Christianity in Asia Minor depends on him.

Crete

In contrast to Ephesus, we know nothing of the origins of Christianity in Crete, nor do we know in which part of the 150-mile-long island Titus was based. All we hear of the island in Acts is a brief stop on Paul's voyage to Rome in Acts 27:7–13, but Paul was by then a prisoner, and there is no sign either of any opportunity to evangelize or of a Christian community already in existence. We can only assume that after his release from prison Paul had been able to begin the work of founding churches on the island (Crete is only some 200 miles from Ephesus), and had left Titus to look after them, as he did Timothy at Ephesus.

This would, then, be a much younger church even than that at Ephesus at the time when Paul wrote his letter to Titus: Titus 1:5 seems to refer to the first appointment of elders ('bishops') after the churches were established, whereas at Ephesus the church had been going for ten years or more, and we have already met its elders in Acts 20:17. But the problems of the church in Crete, as we can discern them from Paul's letter, seem on the whole quite similar to those of its older sister, though there is not quite the same sense of urgency over the threat of false teaching.

In these letters, then, we shall witness the teething troubles of young churches in a setting very remote from our own. In the next study we shall think about how we may expect to learn from them, before we turn to the text in detail.

PRAYER

Thank you, Lord, for those men and women of faith and courage who long ago preached the gospel and set your Church on its journey. May we who follow them have the same faith and courage to meet the very different challenges of our generation. Amen.

2 1 & 2 TIMOTHY; TITUS

WHAT HAS IT GOT *to* DO *with* US?

The 'usefulness' of scripture

Paul wrote to Timothy that 'all scripture is inspired by God and is useful for teaching, for reproof, for correction, and for training in righteousness' (2 Timothy 3:16). He was not talking about his own letters, of course, but about those Hebrew sacred writings that Timothy had known from childhood, which we call the Old Testament. But in the time of Paul and Timothy those writings from the ancient Hebrew world must have seemed just as 'foreign' and out of date as Paul's own letters might seem to us today. None the less, Paul believed that they had a timeless quality and a relevance to practical Christian discipleship which transcended the time and circumstances of their original writing. And the Church has felt the same about Paul's own letters, which is why we now have them in our Bibles.

But using these letters as guidance for Christian living and thinking today can be tricky. Our churches are not very like the churches in Ephesus and Crete in the 60s of the first century, and the challenges we face are not the same. Paul's letters deal with the specific questions and crises of those local churches, and we cannot always simply assume that he would have said the same thing to us in our very different circumstances.

An example: the 'silencing' of women

Probably the most controversial example is Paul's robust words about the ministry of women in 1 Timothy 2:11–12: women are not to teach or to exercise authority over men. Yet not only in wider society but also in many of the Christian churches today women are treated (at least in theory) as equal with men, and they are ordained to positions of teaching and responsibility in many churches. Must we then conclude that Paul would never have allowed this, and a church which does so must either boldly assert that Paul (or whoever wrote those words) was simply wrong, or live with a bad conscience if it claims to be guided by the New Testament?

But these were letters written for a specific time and place, and our knowledge of what was going on is quite limited. Was there perhaps some particular local problem about what women were getting up to in Ephesus? Had it anything to do with the influence of the Temple of Artemis which was run by women and eunuchs? Or was a particular group of women in the Ephesian church proving to be a nuisance to the church leadership (see Paul's comments on the younger widows in 1 Timothy 5:11–15)? Should we give weight to the fact that Paul wants women first to 'learn' (1 Timothy 2:11)? But when they *have* 'learned', what then? Are they still forbidden to teach?

All these and many other such arguments have been used to suggest that what Paul was giving in 1 Timothy 2:11–12 was not a ruling in principle for all time, but guidance on a specific local and probably temporary problem. When we take into account the quite extensive evidence in the rest of the New Testament for the prominent role of women in the Christian mission and in at least some churches (including Paul's own churches), some such conclusion seems necessary.

What are we looking for?

Should we then be looking not so much for unchanging regulations as for principles which need to be applied in new ways to new situations? Ought we to try to trace developments within New Testament thinking, and aim to plot their trajectories so as to discover how the same values and principles should be applied to our different world and time? If we insist that Paul's words about women's ministry in 1 Timothy 2:11–12 must be applied literally today, why do we not draw the same conclusion with regard to his much more extensive instructions for the treatment of widows in 1 Timothy 5:3–16?

This was just one example of a problem which will crop up in different ways as we read these letters. There is no simple and universal answer, and it is not surprising that Christians sometimes come to different conclusions. But it is important at the outset to be aware that reading off answers for today from letters of the first century is not always as straightforward a business as it may seem.

PRAYER

Lord, help us to be honest about our uncertainties, and humble about our differences. Help us to seek eagerly for the 'teaching, reproof, correction and training' of your word, and forgive us when we get it wrong! Amen.

3

1 TIMOTHY 1:1–7

A DAUNTING TASK

A chain of command

Paul's letters are never trivial. Even the opening greeting in verses 1–2 is full of food for thought.

Paul himself is a man under authority. He has received his command from the highest authority of all, and it is that conviction which governs all his life and work. He is under orders from 'God our Saviour and Christ Jesus our hope'. Would you have thought of describing Jesus like that?

But he in turn has authority, because God has appointed him an apostle, and again and again in his letters he reminds people of the fact. So he is writing to Timothy not merely with advice but with instructions, which he expects to be followed without question.

Timothy is not only his deputy, he is also Paul's 'child in the faith' (v. 2). He became a Christian when Paul first visited his home town, Lystra in Asia Minor (Acts 14:5–21), and Paul soon took him on as his travelling companion and helper (Acts 16:1–3). So Paul became his spiritual father, and loved and trusted him more than all his other associates. Now that trust has led him to place on his 'loyal child' a task which will test his loyalty to the limit.

Stopping the rot

Paul's last visit to Ephesus has left him anxious. Instead of concentrating on the wholesome Christian teaching which promotes good living, some people in the church at Ephesus (and very likely among its appointed elders) have become preoccupied with 'myths and endless genealogies' (v. 4) which are undermining their effectiveness as Christians. So when Paul had to move on northwards, he left Timothy behind to control this 'meaningless talk', and to recall the members of the church to basics.

We are not told just what these strange ideas were which worried Paul so much. In 4:7 he will refer to them again as 'profane myths and old wives' tales', and Titus is apparently facing similarly damaging teaching in Crete (Titus 1:14; 3:9), where Paul speaks specifically of Jewish myths and quarrels about the law. In some Jewish circles at that time, there were quite extravagant speculations about the cosmos and its origins and about the angels and powers of the unseen world, and it may be that Christians in Ephesus were buying into some of this fascinating pseudo-philosophy. We do not have to look far in our day to find people caught up in similarly irresponsible currents of thought, which easily divert their energies from the things which matter.

So instead of building up their own and other people's faith by sound teaching, they are dissipating their energies in silly nonsense. Worse still, they want to be thought of as 'teachers of the law' (v. 7), even though they don't know what they are talking about. With such leaders, the church will quickly lose its way. It is up to Timothy to stop the rot.

Good teaching promotes good living

It is not just a matter of intellectual disagreement. Paul is at heart a pastor, concerned for how his people live. The 'sound teaching' to which he will constantly refer in these letters not only corrects people's ideas, but guides their lives. Look at verse 5 for a proper sense of priorities. It is that sort of good living ('love', 'a pure heart', 'a good conscience', 'sincere faith') which is the test of good teaching, and which is in danger of being sacrificed in the search for intellectual novelties. If the church in Ephesus is to live up to its calling as the people of God, it depends on Timothy to rescue it from these misguided enthusiasts.

FOR REFLECTION

What sort of 'different doctrines' threaten the Church today, and how are they best confronted? In what ways can we apply to our situation the test that good teaching produces good living?

Law & Gospel

What the law is for

Paul seems to have had a love–hate relationship with the law. By 'law' he means primarily the law of Moses as it is laid down in the Old Testament, but often along with this goes the whole principle of 'law-keeping' which derived from it, and which by his time had resulted in a massive expansion of the original Old Testament law by rabbinic commentaries and regulations to try to bring every aspect of life under the rule of the law.

And the law in this latter sense could be an enemy of the gospel. Paul's letters to the Galatians and to the Romans are full of the danger of trying to find salvation by simply observing the law. It is futile, he says, not only because no one can in fact match up to the full demands of the law, but also because to try to do so is to miss the real way of salvation which God has provided through faith in Christ. So he can rejoice in being 'free from the law', and can call on his readers to resist any attempt to bring them back under 'slavery' to it (Galatians 3:23–26; 5:1, 18).

Yet the law of Moses was, Paul believed, the word of God: 'the law is good' (v. 8). And so of course that law could never be evil (Paul discusses this in Romans 7:7–14). So the problem could not be with the law itself, but rather with how it is used. That is the point which Paul picks up here. The problem with the would-be 'teachers of the law' he has spoken of in verse 7 is that they do not understand what the law is for.

The translation 'innocent' (v. 9, NRSV) is misleading. The word is 'righteous', which is the word Paul uses not for people who behave blamelessly but for those who have found, through faith in Christ, a 'righteousness not from the law' (Philippians 3:9). Such people have found salvation apart from the law, and for them the law is no longer a master. Its function is rather to restrain the wickedness of those who have not found 'righteousness by faith', and who must be kept under control.

A catalogue of vice

The list in verses 9–10 of behaviour which is 'contrary to sound teaching' makes dismal reading. These, Paul implies, are the sort of things people get up to when they are not under God's control. It is a deliberately extreme catalogue: murder of father or mother is hardly an everyday occurrence even in the most godless society! But these are the lengths to which human depravity can go, and it is the concern of God's law to restrain them.

Most of the items, however lurid, are fairly self-explanatory. But the inclusion of 'sodomites' in the list draws attention these days. This is one of the half-dozen places in the Bible where homosexual practice is specifically mentioned as something which God disapproves. The word (which occurs also in a similar list in 1 Corinthians 6:9) means literally 'those who lie with males'. Paul here gives no further explanation of the term, but it seems clearly to reflect the Jewish repudiation of the sort of male homosexual relationships which were common and even approved in Greek and Roman society. Paul's views on homosexuality are more fully spelled out in Romans 1:24–32. The Bible does not have a lot to say directly on the subject, but the biblical writers are consistent in upholding heterosexual relations as the way God intended sex to be. We should note, however, that this is just one item in a list which also includes such vices as lying and perjury; it is one vice among many, not singled out for special attention.

Sound teaching

It is a relief to turn from this list in verses 9–10 to the 'glorious gospel' in verse 11. This 'good news' (which is the literal meaning of 'gospel') has been the mainspring of Paul's great life's work. It is not just a truth to be believed, an intellectual grasp of God's plan and purpose. It is a whole new way of life, within which the unattractive behaviour he has just listed has no place. 'Sound teaching' produces sound living, because it has its origin in none other than the 'blessed God' to whose service both Paul and Timothy, and those whom they serve, are committed.

PRAYER

Help us, Lord, so to absorb the 'sound teaching' of the gospel that we may be free from the rule of law, and our lives may proclaim the good news to others. Amen.

5 1 TIMOTHY 1:12–17

Paul's Testimony

Paul's past

From the point of view of his position as a Christian believer and leader of the church, Paul's life before he met Jesus on the Damascus road qualified him well for the title of 'foremost of sinners' (v. 15). His friend Luke illustrates graphically his record as a 'persecutor and man of violence' against the early believers in Jesus (Acts 8:3; 9:1–2, 13–14). As for 'blaspheming', that depends on where you are looking from: his repudiation of Jesus and his determination to stamp out the new movement would seem from the Christian point of view the ultimate blasphemy.

But for Paul at the time it was not so. He genuinely believed that Jesus was an impostor, and that it was his duty as a pious Jew to stamp out the new and misguided cult. The pious end justified the violent means (as it has so often in the history of religious persecution). Paul, like all fanatics, was utterly sincere and single-minded in his pursuit of what he believed to be right. That is why, he believes, God had mercy on him. He was acting 'ignorantly in unbelief', and God's mercy consisted not in condoning that ignorance, but in shattering his unbelief.

Paul was a man of extremes: at one moment the chief threat to the early Christian movement, at the next its chief protagonist and most effective missionary. As such, he is an example, even if an extreme one, of what God can do, of the grace and power of the gospel (v. 16).

Paul's gospel

The phrase 'The saying is sure' (v. 15) will occur again in 3:1; 4:9; 2 Timothy 2:11 and Titus 3:8 to mark key pronouncements which Paul wants to be noticed and remembered. Here it takes us to the heart of the good news, that there is salvation for sinners, even for the worst. A remarkable sequence of nouns in these verses spells out something of what that has meant for Paul himself: in Christ he has experienced God's 'mercy', 'grace', 'faith', 'love', 'patience'. In the face of the utmost provocation that a human being could offer to him, God has responded with nothing but kindness and understanding, and that grace has prevailed and changed Paul's life for ever. So now instead of the judgment that he so richly deserved, Paul, together with all who have believed in Jesus, can look forward to 'eternal life' (v. 16).

And not only has Christ 'saved' him. He has also given him a new direction for his previously misguided zeal. Amazingly, this would-be destroyer of the Church has been 'judged faithful and appointed to Christ's service' (v. 12), and with the 'strengthening' that Christ has given he has been able to share his experience of God's grace with countless others who, if less spectacular in their wickedness, were no less in need of the good news that 'Christ Jesus came into the world to save sinners' (v. 15). You could hardly have a more convincing testimony to God's love and power than this 'poacher turned game-keeper'.

Paul's praise

One of the attractive features of Paul's letters is his tendency sometimes to break off into a shout of praise (after which he comes back to earth and gets on with the letter!). Here in verse 17 he cannot contain his excitement as he recalls how good God has been to him, and the sheer wonder of such a gospel of salvation. God is beyond all human measure, incomparable and unfathomable. The right response to such a being, in his gracious dealing with his human creation, is not intellectual analysis but praise, 'honour and glory for ever and ever'.

PRAYER

Fill thou my life, O Lord my God,
in every part with praise;
that my whole being may proclaim
thy being and thy ways.

Horatius Bonar (1808–89)

6 1 TIMOTHY 1:18–20

FIGHT *the* GOOD FIGHT

Timothy's commission

Paul has been digressing. His mention of the would-be teachers of the law in verse 7 led him into some thoughts about the role of the law (vv. 8–10), and that in turn led him to reflect on the grace of God which had delivered him from the punishment which he lawfully deserved (vv. 11–17).

Now he returns to the purpose of the letter, which was to give Timothy his instructions for the crucial task he has been left in Ephesus to carry out (vv. 3–7). In chapter 2 those instructions will begin, but first Paul offers some further comments to strengthen Timothy's resolve.

He reminds him first of some earlier prophecies. We do not know exactly what these were, but it seems reasonable to connect them with Timothy's public commissioning for leadership, which took place 'through prophecy' (4:14). At that time the laying on of the hands of the church's elders marked a 'gift' which Timothy had received, presumably the gift needed to enable him to lead the local church once Paul had left. The prophetic utterance on that occasion no doubt related to that gift. So Paul now reminds him of the prophecy both to reassure him that it is God who has called him to his role of leadership and has equipped him for it, and also to reinforce his sense of the importance of the task which has been entrusted to him by God himself.

The Christian soldier's armour

'Fight the good fight' (v. 18) is a metaphor which Paul will later use to describe his own completed ministry (2 Timothy 4:7). These days we are a bit sensitive about military metaphors (a recent hymn book has rewritten 'Onward Christian soldiers' as 'Onward Christian pilgrims'!) but Paul had no such inhibitions, and his life's experience was of a constant battle for the truth, a battle not only against other people but against the more ultimate forces of evil (Ephesians 6:10–17). Timothy must expect no less, and with the church's prophetic backing he will be able to maintain his stand.

His weapons are not those of worldly warfare, but 'faith and a good conscience'. Faith keeps everything in perspective (see the comments on Hebrews 11:1 later in this book). 'We walk by faith, not by sight,' says Paul in 2 Corinthians 5:7. To the person of faith God is real, and the unseen world of spiritual reality more important than the human and environmental pressures which surround us day by day. And a 'good conscience', a life lived according to God's standards, is an essential supplement to faith. Thus armed in mind and behaviour, Timothy will be well equipped to fight a good fight for God.

A sobering warning

There are those in Ephesus who have failed in this. Hymenaeus will reappear in 2 Timothy 2:17, and Alexander may well be the same person who is mentioned as a troublemaker again in 2 Timothy 4:14. Paul speaks as if they have been members of the church, but have now turned against it. The vivid metaphor of shipwreck indicates a complete collapse of their former Christian profession.

Paul cannot treat such apostasy lightly, and he has exercised his apostolic authority in 'turning them over to Satan'. The same phrase is used in 1 Corinthians 5:5, where the church as a whole is expected to discipline a notorious sexual offender in this way. It looks like a formal excommunication. But both here and in 1 Corinthians 5:5 it is apparently not simply a repudiation of the offender, but an attempt to bring them to repentance and restoration. For the true pastor, discipline is not a means of punishment so much as of care for those who are in spiritual danger.

Faced with such a sombre example, Timothy will need to maintain carefully his own 'faith and good conscience' if he is to fight a good fight.

FOR REFLECTION

Are we in danger of taking too lightly the biblical idea of 'spiritual warfare'?

Is there any place for discipline to be exercised over church members who fail today? How might it be done in such a way as to restore the one who has failed?

7 1 TIMOTHY 2:1–7

PRAYER COMES FIRST

Praying for everyone

It is remarkable that, with so many problems in the church at Ephesus, Paul begins his instructions to Timothy not with 'trouble-shooting' but with the central importance of prayer—and not with Timothy's personal prayer life but with the public prayers of the church, not for their own immediate concerns but for the world at large. Most of us today, both in our personal and in our corporate prayer, could learn a lot from this sense of priority.

'Supplications, prayers, intercessions, and thanksgivings' (v. 1) is an impressive phrase, not so much defining different types of prayer (though note the inclusion of 'thanksgiving' along with prayers of request), but underlining that prayer is to be taken seriously and should feature prominently in the gatherings of the church.

Nor is it to be simply for the church's own domestic concerns. It is to be 'for everyone' (v. 1). But because all our lives are so closely affected by the political structures within which we live, and by the people who control them, it is especially appropriate that we pray for those in authority, not only for their own sakes but so that through their exercise of that authority the life of everyone may be 'quiet and peaceable' (v. 2).

It is not just international peace that concerns Paul (in the Roman Empire, that was not so pressing an issue as it may be today) but the general quality of life. That is God's concern, and must be the concern of his people. There is no conflict between commitment to the gospel and a wider concern for the whole of life. Indeed Paul's phrase 'godliness and dignity' (v. 2) succinctly blends the religious and social aspects of life in a single harmonious ideal.

God's universal purpose

We pray for everyone because God cares for everyone. More specifically, he wants everyone to be saved (v. 4). This is the basis of Paul's mission, and of his indefatigable labours as a 'herald and apostle' (v. 7). Any theology which restricts the grace of God by excluding any nation, type or social class of people from the scope of the good news has missed the point. If the gospel is truth (note the repetition of this word in verses 4 and 7) then it is truth for everyone, and everyone needs to hear it and respond. That is God's great desire, and it should be equally the passion of his people.

If the gospel is for everyone and is the truth, then there is only one gospel, only one way to find the grace of God. In these days when many voices tell us that Christians have no right to try to impose their religious beliefs on people of other faiths and philosophies, we need to ponder carefully the implications of Paul's words in verses 5–6. These verses have a rhythmic structure, and may well be drawn from a creed or hymn expressing the basic belief of the early Church. They are clear and uncompromising.

It is not only that there is only one God (on that many religions and philosophies could agree), but that access to that one God is by means of a unique mediator. In drawing attention specifically to Jesus' humanity, Paul is not wishing to question the belief that he is God (for which see, within these letters, 3:16 and Titus 2:13), but emphasizing his unique place as divine and yet at the same time 'one of us'. Moreover, only Jesus has given himself as a 'ransom' (see his own words in Mark 10:45); it is only through the cross that reconciliation is achieved between God and his people. So there can be no other mediator, and that ransom must be not for a selected few but 'for all'. There is no other.

PRAYER

Pray for everyone, but especially for 'rulers and all who are in high positions'. Pray especially for the free proclamation of the one gospel which everyone needs to hear and to respond to.

8 1 TIMOTHY 2:8–10

MEN & WOMEN *at* PRAYER

How men should pray

'Men' here (v. 8) means males, not just 'people'. It is assumed that they will take the lead in the church's public prayers. Such an assumption would cause no surprise in Paul's day, when women's role in public life was, with rare exceptions, to be seen and not heard. But it is interesting to observe that already in the Corinthian church it had become normal for women also to be heard praying (1 Corinthians 11:5); the progressive recognition of the equal value of women in God's sight, for which the Christian Church was at least partly responsible, had already begun.

The lifting of the hands was a traditional Jewish and Christian gesture of prayer. Paul's point here is not necessarily to prescribe the mode of prayer, but rather that the hands which are (as a matter of fact) lifted up in prayer should be holy hands. It is the character of the one praying which matters. Positively it is to be one of holiness; negatively there is to be no anger or argument. In the light of 1:4–7; 4:1–3 and 6:3–5, this seems to have been an appropriate warning for the Ephesian church. It's not much good praying for a 'quiet and peaceable life' (v. 2) if you can't get on with your fellow Christians without wrangling and bad temper!

What about the women?

'Also' (v. 9, NRSV) is literally 'likewise', and it is quite likely that Paul means that the women too should be praying publicly just like the men (as they did in Corinth). Presumably he would want them to share the same attitude of holiness and peaceableness which he expects of the men, but the focus of his specific instructions for them is rather on their appearance, which is to be decent and appropriate. Peter has some similar comments to make about how women should dress and what constitutes true attractiveness for a Christian woman (1 Peter 3:3–4).

In the Greek and Roman world, female cosmetics could be very elaborate and expensive. The gold and pearls may have been worn as jewellery, but are quite likely to have been part of an elaborate hairdo, with the hair braided in layers with jewels and gold between. (The Roman satirist Juvenal describes women whose outrageous hairstyles involve 'numerous tiers and storeys piled one upon another on her head'!) The object of such flamboyant dressing is at least to draw attention, and the danger is always that it could be sexually provocative. What Paul wants to see rather is 'modesty and decency'. The adornment he approves is not visual display but 'good works'. (1 Peter 3:4 makes much the same point.)

Such passages in the Bible have been taken by some as a prohibition of any sort of beauty aids. But that is to miss the point of Paul's instruction. He is not giving timeless rules about women's dress code which can be applied literally to any culture, but trying to promote an appropriate atmosphere for corporate prayer. The 'holiness' he has required on the part of the men who are praying is not to be undermined by the distraction of women who flaunt their charms in the place of prayer. And the women's own reverence in prayer is hardly compatible with making a bid for male attention.

There may well have been special cause for concern in Ephesus, where women played a leading role in the worship of Artemis and sexual activity was apparently an integral part of that worship. Paul wants to make sure that the Christian community in Ephesus sets a different example, and that its prayers are appropriately holy and decent to suit their reverence for a holy God. It is for us in our different situations to work out what are the right ways of expressing and promoting such reverence in our own public worship.

FOR REFLECTION

What are the things that get in the way of your 'holy' approach to God in prayer, or that may distract you from reverent worship? How can they be remedied?

9 1 TIMOTHY 2:11–15

The SILENCING *of* WOMEN

A problem passage

In Study 2, I offered some preliminary thoughts about the problems of interpreting this little paragraph. It is the one and only passage in the New Testament which explicitly forbids women to exercise an authoritative and teaching ministry in the Church, and it has therefore not surprisingly been at the centre of recent discussion of the ministry of women. I have discussed it at some length in *Women in the Church's Ministry* (Paternoster, 1995, pp. 56–72).

The danger is that this passage is sometimes taken in isolation from the rest of the New Testament, and given a normative force of its own. When we see that in the churches under Paul's authority women did in fact exercise a varied and responsible ministry, apparently including teaching and authority even over men, it is clear that such an approach will not do. Paul's friend Priscilla (see Acts 18:26; Romans 16:3–4) does not seem to have operated under the restrictions of 1 Timothy 2:11–15!

A local difficulty?

The irresponsible behaviour of some younger widows at Ephesus (5:11–15) perhaps points us in the right direction. In a city dominated by the worship of Artemis, with its strongly sexual connotations and its leadership by eunuchs and women, these 'liberated' young women posed a problem for the church. When they set themselves up as teachers, without having any grounding in Christian truth (1:6–7), Timothy must beware and take firm action.

There were some strands of Gnostic teaching which turned Eve from a weak and gullible victim into a heroine, standing for the liberation of humanity from superstition. Some even taught that she was created before Adam. There were even those who worshipped the serpent, as the source of enlightenment! Paul's words in verses 13–14 may well be aimed at some such perversion of biblical teaching which was current among these Ephesian women.

'Let her learn'

Whatever the exact nature of the local problem, Paul's concern is focused on the need of these women to 'learn' rather than to teach. He does not say what is to happen if and when they have been sufficiently instructed to become potential teachers in the Christian church. At the time of writing, that probably seems too remote a possibility for Paul to need to give Timothy any guidance on it yet. But a glance at what Paul says about some of his female fellow workers in Romans 16:1–16, and especially at what we know from elsewhere about the activities of one of them, Priscilla, suggests that the ban on teaching may not have been meant to be permanent.

But Paul is concerned not only about the ignorance of these women, but also their attitude. 'Have authority' (v. 12) translates a rare and strong word, better rendered 'domineer' or 'dictate'. It is the opposite of the quiet and respectful attitude which he here calls for. As the NRSV notes indicate, the words here for 'woman' and 'man' are also used more specifically for 'wife' and 'husband', and it is possible that Paul is here concerned particularly about the attitude of wives to their husbands rather than the more general relations of women to men in the church. Was this why he felt it appropriate that younger widows should get back into a family situation (5:14)?

Adam and Eve

So Paul reminds Timothy of the original family, and of the trouble which was caused when Eve stepped out of line and Adam followed. As a result, childbearing became hazardous, and the marriage relationship lost its original harmony (Genesis 3:16). But all is not lost. If these Ephesian women can return to their wifely role and promote a healthy marriage relationship through their faith, love, holiness and modesty, the dire effects of Eve's ill-judged gesture of defiance can be mitigated. Some such sequence of thought probably best accounts for Paul's enigmatically brief comment on the first marriage.

FOR REFLECTION

How far should our interpretation and use of a biblical passage be limited by the circumstances of its original writing? How should we relate Paul's injunctions here to our experience of women's ministry today?

10 1 TIMOTHY 3:1–7

QUALIFICATIONS *for* CHURCH LEADERSHIP

See the Introduction (pp. 15–16) for the meaning of 'bishops'. They were apparently the same as 'elders', a group of local church members appointed to leadership (not like our 'bishops' today). Timothy apparently had the responsibility for their appointment.

A noble task

Something of the significance of the work of elders/bishops in the early Christian churches may be understood from Peter's charge to the elders of the churches in Asia Minor in 1 Peter 5:1–4: it is no less than 'tending the flock of God' (1 Peter 5:2) and those who do it well can look forward to an unfading crown of glory from the Chief Shepherd. Such a task is not to be undertaken lightly, nor entrusted to those who are not fitted for it.

Above reproach

The first qualification given, in verse 2, is picked up again in the last (v. 7). People will judge the church by its leaders. They may sometimes criticize unjustly, but at any rate the way the leaders live must offer no handle for criticism. Paul specifically mentions their reputation among 'outsiders', and the qualities he lists in verses 2 and 3 are the sort of moral standards which should be respected by anyone whatever their creed. People who live like this will always commend the gospel, whereas to incur 'disgrace' over such matters is a 'snare of the devil', in that it gives him the advantage over the people of God.

Most of the qualities listed are obvious enough: 'above reproach… temperate, sensible… hospitable, an apt teacher' and so on. They are well worth pondering, but need no comment by me. But there are three points which deserve a comment. Two of them concern marriage and family.

A model family?

'Married only once' (v. 2, NRSV) is literally 'the husband of one wife'. It is unlikely that Paul is worried about polygamy, since there is little evidence for it occurring in Greek society. It is also improbable that he wants to rule out those who have married again after being widowed, since he specifically instructs young widows to remarry (5:14). He may well have in mind the multiple partners involved in divorce and remarriage, on which Jesus took such an uncompromising line (Matthew 19:9). But perhaps it is best to understand him as more generally requiring marital faithfulness; you could translate it 'a one-woman man'!

The concern for the would-be leader's family life is further developed in verses 4 and 5: you can judge the man by the way his children behave! That is a test few of us would feel entirely comfortable with, and yet it has the ring of common sense as Paul draws the obvious conclusion that a man who cannot lead his own family is not likely to be more successful with the bigger and potentially more unruly family of the church.

Christian maturity

Verse 6—'he must not be a recent convert'—is another shrewd observation. There is something attractive about the zeal and commitment of many a new convert, and it might seem a good idea to harness these qualities into the leadership of the church. But experience shows that too much responsibility too soon can go to a person's head, and if that happens the devil will be delighted.

Paul's advice to Timothy about the selection of 'bishops' is full of good sense. If it rules out some exciting but risky appointments, it ensures that the church will be in good, safe hands. History, including recent history, records many examples of inappropriate leadership, and all too often the result is scandal which damages the credibility of the gospel among outsiders. That is Paul's great concern.

FOR REFLECTION

Think of Christian leaders whom you have most admired, and see how they match up to these criteria. Are you 'Christian leadership material'? If not, why not?

11 1 TIMOTHY 3:8–13

MORE *about* LEADERSHIP

'Deacons' (the word means 'servant') were apparently a second tier of ministry in the Church, less prominent than the 'bishops', but still exercising an important role, mainly at a more practical level. Paul offers similar instructions about the qualifications needed, but there are some interesting additional points included.

Together with the deacons, he mentions 'women' (v. 11). The fact that they, like bishops and deacons, must meet certain tests of character suggests that he is talking about a particular group, not just women in general, but we do not have enough information to decide just who they were. They may be women deacons, or the wives of male deacons, or perhaps women with some more specific ministry of their own.

Serious and sober

Both deacons and women are to be 'serious' (vv. 8, 11): the word means something like 'worthy of respect', or 'dignified', the sort of person others can look up to. In particular Paul is concerned about the way they talk: 'not double-tongued' and 'not slanderers' both focus on the danger of thoughtless gossip about other people. A Christian official must be someone whose talk you can trust, someone who respects confidences, and in whose hands your reputation is safe.

Just as Paul referred to the danger of would-be bishops being drunkards and called for them to be 'temperate' (the word refers primarily to not being drunken), so he now makes the same demand of both deacons and women. Paul was no teetotaller (see 5:23), and does not expect the deacons to abstain from alcohol altogether. The danger is when they 'indulge in much wine'. There have been not a few Christian workers whose ministry has been compromised in this area. An ability to use alcohol responsibly without being under its control is not only a necessity in itself, but also a sign of the sort of stable character which Paul is looking for in those who are entrusted with Christian responsibility.

Faith and a good conscience

Timothy's own leadership of the church depends on maintaining 'faith and a good conscience' (1:19), but even for the deacons, whose tasks were probably much less high-profile and more mundane, these are equally vital qualities. The Christian faith is a 'mystery' (v. 9) not in our English sense that it is hard to understand, but rather as a secret, available only to those who are let into it. The same word is rightly translated 'secret' in Mark 4:11. Deacons are people who have discovered for themselves the secret of God's grace through Christ, and who now hold it fast as the basis of their life and teaching. The 'clear conscience' (v. 9) is as important as the intellectual grasp of the truth.

Passing the test

Just as bishops must be mature Christians, not new converts, so also deacons must be tested before their ministry is approved (vv. 10 and 13). The testing is presumably by training on the job with other church leaders. As they are seen to be doing it well, they will receive further responsibility. And just as the role of bishop is a 'noble task' (3:1), so good service as a deacon (and remember that the word means 'servant') brings 'good standing' and 'great boldness in the faith'. Jesus had taught that those who wish to be first among his disciples must be the servants of all, and that scale of values is reflected here. Honour is to be found not by aiming for high-profile positions, but by doing a good job in the role to which you have been called. Such faithful service will be noticed and respected. And those who serve well will enjoy that good conscience which is the basis for Christian confidence before God and boldness in his service.

There is something wonderfully wholesome about these apparently down-to-earth instructions for Timothy as he supervises Christian ministry at Ephesus, and takes care that only those who are sufficiently mature and responsible are called to lead the church. You could be confident for the future of a church with such leadership.

PRAYER

Thank you, Lord, for the men and women you have called and equipped to lead your Church through the ages. Help our leaders to fulfil these high expectations, and may we honour them as their service deserves. Amen.

12 1 TIMOTHY 3:14–16

The MYSTERY *of* OUR RELIGION

Paul's plans

In the Introduction and Study 1, we have noted that the narrative of Acts does not cover the period when these letters were written, and that all we know of Paul's movements is what we can glean from the letters themselves. It seems that Paul is again free to travel (unlike in 2 Timothy when he is back in prison) and in view of the importance of the Christian presence in Ephesus, the capital of Asia, it is not surprising that he would plan to visit there to support Timothy in his leadership (v. 14). But travel plans in the ancient Mediterranean world could never be taken for granted, and so this letter is designed to fill the gap if he is unable to get there as soon as he hopes.

The importance of the Church

The thought of the responsibility he has left Timothy to fulfil prompts Paul to some powerful words both about the church (v. 15) and about the gospel (v. 16).

The church which Timothy has been left to lead is not just a voluntary human organization, a club of like-minded people with a taste for religion. It operates on a different level altogether, the level of God and truth. It is God's 'household' or family, the community of those who through faith in Christ have entered into a personal relationship with God as their Father and so with one another as brothers and sisters. In such a family, quite different standards and expectations will apply from those of normal human society, and it is Timothy's task to promote that different behaviour.

And this is no mere make-believe, for it is the church of 'the living God'. This powerful little phrase occurs only a few times in Old and New Testaments, but wherever it occurs it carries a sense of expectation. This God is not a pious figment or a philosophical abstraction, but a God who is real and who acts decisively in his world. To be involved with the living God is to be in touch with ultimate reality, and you cannot know him and leave your life unaffected.

God can stand up for himself. But he has chosen to be represented on earth by the Church, a gathering of fallible people who, because of the God who has called them, stand for his truth. 'Pillar and bulwark' (v. 15) suggests a solidity and reliability beyond the reach of any human institution; but for all the faults of the Church as we know it, it is here that people must be in touch with the truth, and it is the Church's responsibility to defend it. That is why the Church matters.

An early Christian creed?

In verse 16, even more obviously than in 2:5–6, Paul seems to be quoting, probably from a hymn or a creed recited in the church. It sets out the 'mystery' ('secret', see comments on 3:9) of the Christian faith in the form of a succinct summary of the story of Jesus, a gospel in a nutshell. The rhythmic clauses tell of his incarnation, his resurrection ('vindicated in spirit') and his return to heaven in glory (compare the pattern of another 'hymn' in Philippians 2:6–11). This amazing story has not only been witnessed by the angels, but has also been proclaimed among human beings, even among those who were formerly outside the people of God. And as they have heard, so they have believed. Thus heaven and earth are united in praise and worship of the incarnate and ascended Son of God.

It is an astonishingly bald summary, and all of us no doubt would have wanted to add many other clauses to it, particularly with reference to the atoning work of Jesus. But, brief as it is, it conveys a sense of wonder and of the supreme importance of the message of Jesus. A church called to witness to this unique truth is in a privileged position indeed.

FOR REFLECTION

Think about the terms in which Paul summarizes the gospel in verse 16. Are these the sort of items we would have focused on? Is the Church today in danger of trivializing its own message? Would most people recognize it as 'the Church of the living God'?

13 1 TIMOTHY 4:1–5

DANGEROUS DELUSIONS

One of Timothy's main tasks is to confront false teaching in the church in Ephesus, and Paul now turns directly to this issue. He does not mince his words!

The character of the false teachers

Timothy should not be surprised that such problems are arising, since it has been predicted by 'the Spirit' (v. 1). This probably refers to prophetic messages received in the church, though it could refer to Paul's own spiritual perception (as indeed he had earlier expressed it to the elders from Ephesus in Acts 20:29–30). Wherever God is at work, his servants need to be on the alert for satanic perversions of the truth.

And these teachers, apparently members of the church community, are under the influence of spiritual powers hostile to God. Like Eve (see 2:14), they are listening to the voice of Satan rather than to God and are teaching other people accordingly. Paul's words about them in verse 2 could be understood to mean that they are deliberately teaching what they know to be untrue (which is what we mean by 'liars'), but it is more likely that he sees them as the dupes of Satan, peddling untruth in the mistaken belief that, in good Gnostic fashion, they have discovered the real hidden truth. The word 'hypocrisy' in the Gospels (for example, Matthew 15:7; 23:23) generally refers not so much to those who set out to deceive as to those whose viewpoint is so fatally distorted that they cannot grasp the truth.

The phrase about 'consciences seared with a hot iron' (v. 2) probably means that they have been 'cauterized' to the extent that their moral judgments are now radically impaired. It could also carry the image of being 'branded' by Satan as belonging to his flock. Certainly as far as Paul is concerned, whatever their Christian profession, they have in effect 'renounced the faith'.

What they are teaching

The 'teaching' boils down, as so often in the Bible, to a code of conduct. Gnostics regarded the body and all its functions as polluted, aspects of a lower nature which truly 'spiritual' people must learn to overcome. For some Gnostics this could lead to moral licence, on the understanding that what you do with the body has no spiritual significance. For others, and the Ephesian teachers are among them, it led to an extreme asceticism, an attempt to overcome the bodily urges by denying them—perhaps in reaction to the sexual freedom around them. For such people (as, sadly, for many Christians since), sex and marriage are dirty, and a truly spiritual life can be lived only by sexual abstinence. This sort of teaching (v. 3) probably lies behind a good part of the problems with marriage which continually resurface in this letter. And the same applies to food.

What God has created is good

Paul's response to this Gnostic asceticism is robust and wholesome. To reject God's creations of sex and food is an insult to the Creator, whose creation was pronounced 'very good' (Genesis 1:31). The true Christian response to these God-given provisions is not embarrassment or shame, but thanksgiving (v. 4). God's gifts are to be enjoyed, not repudiated.

Of course there must be limits to this openness, and in other letters Paul often spells them out. Indeed his lists of vices and virtues in 1:9–10 and 3:2–3 recognize that both sex and food (drink) can be misused. But the object of the moral restrictions is to set us free to enjoy God's gifts in the way he intended, not to withhold them altogether. Where a person's moral standards are determined 'by God's word and by prayer' (v. 5), there need be no fear in enjoying both married life and food and drink with gratitude as the generous gifts of our Creator.

PRAYER

Thank you, God our Creator, for the bodily appetites you have implanted in us. Help us to use them with discretion and with joy, and always to give you thanks for them. Amen.

14 1 TIMOTHY 4:6–10

SPIRITUAL FITNESS

Physical training and godliness

Paul often uses the athlete as a model for taking our Christian discipleship seriously. Even apart from professional athletes, some people spend extraordinary amounts of time, effort and money in seeking physical fitness. Compared with their punishing schedules, how does our care for our spiritual fitness match up? Not that Paul is against physical training—it 'is of some value' (v. 8: more literally, it 'is helpful to a small extent'). But much more important is our training in 'godliness', in living the life of God's people; that is 'helpful for everything'.

The reason for this contrast lies in one of Paul's main themes, the contrast between this (temporary) life on earth and the eternal life to which we look forward through Christ. Physical training, however beneficial, has its pay-off only here on earth: the resurrection body will not be dependent on the fitness of the body that goes to the grave! Spiritual discipline, on the other hand, has its pay-off both here and now (in enabling us to live wholesome, fulfilled, useful lives in God's service) and in the life to come, a life with God for which our growth in 'godliness' now must prepare us. So Timothy is urged to be in training (the verb at the end of verse 7 is that from which we derive 'gymnastics') for eternal life.

Training others

The sort of teaching Paul has outlined in 4:4–5 is essential for the well-being of the Christian brothers and sisters in Ephesus, and Timothy must make sure that he sets it before them. The language (v. 6) suggests serving a meal, and Timothy himself is appropriately described therefore as a 'servant' (the same word as 'deacon' in 3:8, but now in its more basic sense of a domestic servant, here almost a waiter). The metaphor continues with 'nourished'. Timothy himself has been well fed with 'the words of faith and sound teaching' which he has received from Paul, and it is that same wholesome nourishment which he must continue to set before the church as its essential spiritual diet.

Timothy's own training

The spiritual gymnastics which Timothy needs to follow have both negative and positive aspects. Negatively, he is to keep away from the unhealthy diet of 'profane myths and old wives' tales' (v. 7). We are reminded of the language of 1:4–7: 'myths and endless genealogies', 'speculations', 'meaningless talk'. The problem would not go away, and in 2 Timothy 3:1–9 and 4:3–4 he will use even stronger language (note especially 2 Timothy 3:7: 'always being instructed and never arriving at a knowledge of the truth'). In contrast with all this silly nonsense, the simple truth of the gospel and the precepts of Christian morality provide the nourishment which the spiritual athlete needs.

Positively, he is to recognize that fitness is not easily achieved in the spiritual realm any more than in the physical. It involves 'toil and struggle' (v. 10). Christian discipleship is not for those who are looking for the easy life. But, like the strenuous efforts of the mountain climber, it is all worthwhile because of the goal in view. Paul's gospel is one of looking forward, of 'hope'. (Remember 'Christ Jesus our hope' in 1:1?) And that hope is not wishful thinking, because it is based on no less than the 'living God' himself (see comments on 3:15 for the phrase). The ultimate salvation to which we look forward in the life to come, no less than our experience of salvation now, is guaranteed because it is the living God who is our Saviour.

But that salvation, which is intended for all people (see 2:4), is 'especially for those who believe'. Paul's teaching elsewhere forbids us to understand this brief aside as meaning that unbelievers will also be saved. Rather, the salvation which is offered to all is specifically effective for those who believe.

FOR REFLECTION

Think about 'fitness training'. What have we to learn from fitness fanatics? How seriously do you take your 'spiritual gymnastics'?

15 1 TIMOTHY 4:11–16

Look After Yourself

Timothy's effectiveness in leading the church depends on the care with which he develops his own spiritual life and example. Paul knows him well enough to know his potential areas of weakness, and gently encourages him to pay attention to his own discipleship. This is not self-indulgence, but an essential prerequisite for his ministry, for 'in doing this you will save both yourself and your hearers' (v. 16).

Diffidence

At the time of this letter Timothy must have been at least thirty, and it was ten or fifteen years since Paul had recruited him as his associate. He was not the sort of 'recent convert' mentioned in 3:6. But for all his experience he was still a 'youth' (v. 12) in comparison with at least some of the 'elders' over whom he had responsibility, and in a culture which valued the wisdom of age he may well have found it difficult to maintain his authority; indeed some of the people whose teaching he had been appointed to oppose may well have used his age against him.

He is not to be diffident. But it is significant that Paul urges him not so much to assert his delegated authority as Paul's lieutenant but rather to earn its acceptance by the example of his life and speech. It is by the sort of person he is that he will commend his message. There is no answer to love and faith and purity.

The focus of Timothy's ministry

For Paul's planned visit, see 3:14; Timothy's solo responsibility is only for a limited time (v. 13). During that time his essential tasks are 'reading, exhorting and teaching'. NRSV 'the public reading of scripture' represents the single Greek word 'reading'. This assumes that Paul is not talking about Timothy spending time in his study, developing his mind with good books, but reading out 'scripture' to the assembled people. ('Scripture' at this time would mean primarily the Old Testament, though in 5:18 a saying of Jesus is included in a quotation of what 'the scripture says'.) In a church where the majority of members would not be able to read for themselves, this is probably the right interpretation, and the same word is used for the reading aloud of the Old Testament in the synagogues (Acts 13:15; 2 Corinthians 3:14). The exhortation and teaching would follow naturally from such a public reading. The gatherings of the church would therefore be times not only of worship and prayer but also, and perhaps primarily, of learning from the scriptures and from Timothy as their authorized expositor. In the absence of personal pocket Bibles (and the ability to read them), this was the primary source of the 'sound teaching' on which the church's health depended.

Timothy's gift

The word translated 'gift' (v. 14) is *charisma*, the term used in 1 Corinthians 12 for the varied gifts with which the different members of the body of Christ are equipped to enable the whole body to function as it should. In the light of verse 13, it seems likely that it refers here to a gift of teaching ability, enabling Timothy to provide the nurture which the church needs for its health and growth. 'Do not neglect' calls on Timothy both to exercise the gift faithfully rather than letting it lie dormant, and also to foster it, no doubt through his own study of the scriptures as well as through constant practice.

But while it is a divine gift, it has been given to Timothy in connection with prophecy and with the laying on of the hands of the elders. This sounds like a public commissioning at which, in response to a prophetic revelation, the corporate leadership of the church prayed for Timothy to receive the gifts needed for the ministry to which he was being appointed. For a similar combination of elements, see Paul's own commissioning in Acts 13:1–3. From such a beginning, Timothy can press on with confidence to fulfil the divine calling, while the church recognizes in his 'progress' the fulfilment of their prayers.

PRAYER

Help us, Lord, to discern the gifts you have given to us and to others in our church, and to exercise them, each of us for the benefit of all and for your glory. Amen.

CARE *for* WIDOWS

Paul continues to instruct Timothy on the proper regulation of the affairs of the Christian community in Ephesus. Verses 3–16 are concerned with widows—quite a long section and one which reflects the importance of the 'social' agenda for an early Christian community. In a world without State welfare, the care of the elderly and dependent was the responsibility of the family, but it is interesting that the Christian community seems itself to have operated as a large family, taking practical responsibility for its more vulnerable members. Frequent Old Testament references to God's concern for 'orphans and widows' remind us of how insecure life could be for those who lost their immediate family support, and it is taken for granted that God's people will share his concern and turn it into effective practical care.

A pastor's relationships

Before turning specifically to widows, Paul offers in verses 1–2 some general advice on Timothy's relationships with the members of the Christian community, grouped by age and sex. His model is the family, with its tradition of respect for the older members and of love for brothers and sisters. As pastor, Timothy is not to act as the boss (Paul's verb translated 'speak harshly' is a strong one, suggesting bullying), but as a respectful son and brother. Many pastors might benefit from taking this advice for themselves and their ministry! The addition 'with absolute purity' in verse 2 reflects Paul's awareness that Timothy, as a relatively young man, needs to take special care in developing pastoral relationships with younger women as 'sisters', so as to avoid any risk of misunderstanding or of actual sexual involvement (compare 2 Timothy 2:22). It is a risk which all pastors need to take seriously, as experience sadly demonstrates—and as the media love to expose.

Family responsibilities

There are different kinds of widows, and the church's resources must be carefully administered so that help goes where it is most needed and deserved, to those 'who are really widows' (v. 3). Paul will go on to spell out two groups of widows who do not qualify for such help.

First there are those who have families able to look after them (vv. 4, 8, 16), and secondly those who do not meet the criteria set out in 5:9–10, particularly those aged under 60 who are able to remarry and so to find the support of a new household (5:11–15). It also seems to be assumed throughout that it is Christian widows who are in view, not those in the wider society.

The language of verse 8 is very strong. Care for ageing relatives is not an optional act of generosity: it is a fundamental part of Christian discipleship. It is, Paul assumes, only where a widow has no natural family to take care of her that the church's provision should be needed. Today the provision of welfare is different, but it seems reasonable to conclude that if the church's provision for widows in the first century did not excuse the younger members of the family from their primary responsibility, no more does the provision of State welfare in the twenty-first, whether that care is provided in the home or by other appropriate arrangements.

In verses 6–7 Paul further defines a 'real widow' as one who lives for God, not for pleasure. This sounds very dour and puritanical. But Paul is not denouncing simple 'pleasure' as such. The word translated 'live for pleasure' is a rare and strong word implying an extravagant, profligate, debauched lifestyle which could only bring the Christian community into disrepute. The church's resources are not to be used to finance a merry widow's life in the fast lane! The godly widow, on the other hand, is a vital asset to the church; her prayers are indispensable.

FOR REFLECTION

Paul's instructions combine practical concern for the vulnerable with hard-headed realism to ensure that resources are not wasted. Now that we have State welfare, can we find any practical application for Paul's approach? Are there areas of need where the Church should be taking the initiative today as it did for its widows in the first century?

17 1 TIMOTHY 5:9–16

More *about* Widows

The question of who are to be classified as 'real widows' continues in this passage. Clearly Timothy is expected to maintain a list of those who qualify for support from church funds, and Paul expects him to be quite strict in drawing up the list.

Criteria for inclusion on 'the list'

We have considered in the previous study the criterion of whether there is support available from the widow's own family (the issue reappears in verse 16). Now Paul spells out some other qualifications.

Age: Only the over-60s are eligible! That sounds almost like a modern pension scheme, but Paul's concern is apparently with whether the widow may reasonably be expected to marry again and so be supported by a new husband. 'Younger widows' (the under-60s?) should remarry, and by finding a respectable place in society as married women should allow no handle for malicious gossip (v. 14).

Previous marriage: 'Married only once' (v. 9) is the equivalent phrase to what we have discussed in 3:2 and 3:12, and here again the meaning is 'a one-man woman', a phrase which rules out both promiscuousness and divorce and remarriage while the original husband is alive. Presumably it does not rule out remarriage after his death, since in verse 14 Paul *expects* younger widows to remarry, and can hardly intend that by so doing they would automatically disqualify themselves from being classified as 'real widows' if the second husband dies.

Good works: The list of good works in verse 10 is reminiscent of the description of the good wife in Proverbs 31:10–31. All of us, male and female, could ask ourselves how well we would stand up to such a review. Timothy is to take account of the woman's reputation in the local community, and to enrol only those widows who are well spoken of. This is not 'salvation by works', perhaps, but it certainly sanctions a proper reward for the way she has lived. A place in the list of supported widows has to be deserved, and cannot simply be assumed.

The problem with younger widows

Paul's sweeping allegations about younger widows in verses 11–15 presumably reflect worrying reports which he has heard from Ephesus. In the study on 2:11–15, we noted the possibility that it was the uncontrolled behaviour of these younger women which lay behind Paul's drastic ruling against women being allowed to teach in the church in Ephesus. They seem to have no useful work to do, and spend their time getting in other people's way and indulging at best in frivolous and unhelpful talk. If they are the same people Paul had in mind in 1:6–7, the situation is worse. They are setting themselves up as teachers and peddling false ideas. 'Turning away to follow Satan' (v. 15) perhaps points to some such dabbling in dangerous notions. How far this irresponsible behaviour is to be attributed to lack of a stable family situation is not clear, but Paul's desire that they should get married indicates that he feels they would be better behaved if they had husbands!

There is an odd tension between verses 11–12, which speak of a younger widow's own desire to marry as a rejection of Christ and a violation of her 'first pledge', and verse 14 which says they *should* get married again. The solution may be that the 'first pledge' is a pledge of chastity (almost a sort of 'marriage' to Christ?) which was involved in being enrolled as a widow. It is for that reason that Paul deplores the 'sensual desires' (perhaps the sort of flirtatious behaviour we noted in 2:9–10), which might lead them to break that pledge to serve Christ as a widow, and instead to enter an ill-advised marriage. Far better for younger women not to be enrolled as 'widows' at all, but to channel their natural urge into a decent second marriage. That is a possible understanding of Paul's thought here, but it is a pity he has not explained it more clearly!

FOR REFLECTION

In verses 10 and 14 Paul describes some aspects of a wholesome married life. How may these principles be applied to life in our society today?

18 1 TIMOTHY 5:17–22

CHURCH ELDERS

In 3:1–7 we learned about the qualifications needed to serve as a 'bishop' in the church. We have seen in the Introduction that 'bishops' and 'elders' are to be understood as alternative names for the same office of corporate leadership in the local church. Timothy, as Paul's special envoy, is in authority over the elders, responsible for their selection (3:1–7) and 'ordination' (5:22). In this passage we learn also of his responsibility to keep an eye on how they go about their task, and to encourage or correct as may be necessary.

Rewards for good service

The NRSV translation 'who rule well' (v. 17) is misleading. NIV 'who direct the affairs of the church well' would be better. An elder was a leader, but not a 'ruler'. He (or she?) was a member of a team, under the immediate authority of Timothy, whose responsibility it was to direct the affairs of the church. The nature of the task is not further spelled out, except that among the elders it appears that some had a special responsibility for 'preaching and teaching'—which implies that other elders did not preach and teach (see 2:11–12 for Paul's concern that teaching should be only in safe hands). While the preaching and teaching role is apparently the most valued aspect of eldership, Paul's principle of diversity in the body of Christ (1 Corinthians 12) ensures that other gifts are recognized and exercised within the group of elders.

The 'honour' referred to in verse 17 is probably to be understood in specifically financial terms (Greek *time* means both 'honour' and 'price'), since verse 18 is explicitly about payment. This is, then, a rare indication that local church leadership in New Testament times was, at least sometimes, a paid responsibility. Paul insists from time to time on his right to be paid as an itinerant apostle (especially 1 Corinthians 9), even though he has not exercised that right; but the payment of local church leaders is a more far-reaching principle. It may not be a matter of a fixed 'stipend' (so NEB, REB), but some sort of financial recompense is clearly in view, and one which may even be 'performance-related'! The principle is based on 'scripture' by a quotation from Deuteronomy 25:4 (from which Paul also argues for his own right to payment in 1 Corinthians 9:9), which is further reinforced with some words of Jesus (Matthew 10:10; Luke 10:7).

When things go wrong

The church is a human society, and elders, however carefully selected, are fallible. Paul is concerned that Timothy should deal with any lapses with scrupulous fairness, but also firmly and fearlessly. Evidence must be carefully examined (v. 19) and, if well supported, must be brought to the attention of the church as a whole (v. 20), where the person accused will have the opportunity to respond and, if required, to repent. It is vital that Timothy himself remain impartial (v. 21), and therefore he must avoid being involved with any questionable activity so that he himself remains above reproach (v. 22). There is an inevitable element of distance required of the one who may have to decide between conflicting interests. Timothy's life has the potential for being quite lonely.

Paul clearly takes the possibility of failure among the elders very seriously. He is concerned for the health of the church itself, but also for the damage which can be done to the cause of the gospel by bad publicity. It is for this reason that he returns in verse 22 to the issue he broached in 3:6–7, the danger of appointing to leadership those who are not yet ready and tested as mature disciples. The 'laying on of hands' seems to be a sort of 'ordination': Timothy himself had been commissioned in this way (4:14), and he in turn has the task of commissioning elders on behalf of the church. He must exercise this authority with care, aware that he is not just the leader of a human society, but is answerable to 'God, Christ Jesus and the elect angels' (v. 21). Church leadership is not a trivial pursuit!

PRAYER

We thank you, O God, that you have called fallible human beings to carry on your work on earth. We pray for those who are called to lead us, that they may do it well; and may your grace keep them from the failure which would damage the cause of the gospel. Amen.

19 1 TIMOTHY 5:23—6:2

VARIOUS INSTRUCTIONS

As Paul comes towards the end of the letter, a number of shorter paragraphs take up various specific matters of concern.

A little wine

The first concern is with regard to Timothy himself. 1 Timothy 5:23, the classic proof-text of the anti-teetotal lobby, is in fact not about alcohol as such (though it certainly takes its use for granted and approves it), but rather about Timothy's health. We do not know whether Timothy's water-drinking had been a matter of principle (perhaps part of his attempt to 'keep himself pure', v. 22) or simply of taste, but Paul believes that it is contributing to his poor health, and that it is his duty to look after himself. Perhaps pollution in the water supply was part of the problem. A little wine (like the physical exercise Paul has grudgingly commended in 4:8) will help to keep Timothy fit for the work God has called him to do. It is this sort of unstudied personal aside which makes it so hard to read this letter as a literary product for an imagined situation rather than as a real letter displaying one senior Christian's concern for his sickly colleague. 'The very banality of the verse strikes a note of authenticity' (J.N.D. Kelly, *The Pastoral Epistles*, p. 128).

The need for careful discernment

Verses 24–25 are rather cryptic, but probably Paul is returning to the issue of the behaviour of the elders. While some people's sins are blatant, other people's may be less obvious but no less real and no less a cause for ultimate judgment. And the same is true of good behaviour: some are conspicuously good, while with others it may take time for their goodness to come to light. This is probably a warning against superficial, hasty judgment with regard to who are good or bad elders. The wise chief pastor will penetrate below the surface, and discern the good and the bad which have not yet become obvious to everyone.

Slaves and their masters

Paul frequently returns to the question of how Christian slaves should behave (6:1; compare 1 Corinthians 7:21–24; Ephesians

6:5–8; Colossians 3:22–25; Philemon). Here he does not raise the possibility of being set free (1 Corinthians 7:21), but assumes that slaves will remain slaves, even if their masters have also become Christians. It is not the institution of slavery as such that he addresses, but the behaviour appropriate for a Christian slave. And again his overriding concern is that the Christian witness should not be compromised by unacceptable behaviour. Otherwise, God and his gospel will be brought into disrepute.

The proper attitude is one of respect. He does not use the word 'obey', but it seems clear that that is also implied. A Christian slave should be a reliable and good worker. And if the master is also a Christian, far from this condoning the slave in taking liberties, it increases the motivation for conscientious work, since the person for whom they are doing it is not just the boss, but also a fellow member of the Christian community, and therefore the object of their love, not just their respect.

This is remarkable language, which transforms the traditional master–slave relationship into one between 'brothers'. In Paul's letter to Philemon this theme is explored more fully. To us, looking back in the light of the barbarity of the eighteenth-century slave trade and the Christian-inspired campaign for its abolition, it seems inconceivable that Paul could treat slavery so nonchalantly, even when due allowance is made for the much more enlightened treatment of slaves in much of the Roman world. But perhaps in this modest recognition of a Christian slave-owner as a 'brother' and 'beloved' (6:2) we can detect the first traces of the time-bomb which was ultimately to blow apart the very institution which was so unquestioned a part of the world of Paul and Timothy.

FOR REFLECTION

Paul is almost obsessively concerned that the behaviour of Christians should not bring the gospel into disrepute. In what ways might our behaviour cause 'the name of God and the teaching to be blasphemed'?

20 1 TIMOTHY 6:3–10

GODLINESS *with* CONTENTMENT

The main theme of these verses (and one to which Paul will return in 6:17–19) is the Christian's attitude to wealth. In a world which then, as now, was preoccupied with acquiring wealth and the power and comfort it is assumed to guarantee, the different Christian scale of values must have been a striking challenge to people's natural assumptions.

The subject arises, at the end of verse 5, as one example of the perverted attitudes of those who disagree with the 'sound words of our Lord Jesus Christ' which Paul has taught. Such people have appeared earlier in the letter (1:3–7, 19–20; 4:1–3), and Paul is clearly worried about their influence. While Paul's teaching promotes 'godliness' (v. 3), these people foster the most ungodly attitudes and relationships (vv. 4–5). While some allowance must be made for polemical exaggeration, it is important to note that Paul's concern is not mainly that their teaching is intellectually barren, but that it promotes a selfish and destructive lifestyle. As Jesus said, 'You will know them by their fruits' (Matthew 7:16, 20).

A 'prosperity gospel'?

These people thought that 'godliness is a means of gain' (v. 5), and in that they have been followed by many since who have taught that to follow Jesus is a sure route to good health and financial security. Some sects still claim that a Christian has the right to claim from God an affluent and comfortable lifestyle, and that where this is not in evidence it must be the result of sin or lack of faith. It is sometimes called 'prosperity theology', or 'the health and wealth gospel'. This shockingly insensitive doctrine, needless to say, flourishes mainly in the affluent Western world; it would be hard to maintain it in most parts of Africa and Asia, where Christians, however strong their faith, can expect to share the material deprivation of their fellow citizens.

The 'good life'

Paul takes their word 'gain' and turns it on its head. The true 'gain' is in godliness, with contentment. And it is precisely 'contentment' which continues to elude those who understand 'gain' in purely material terms. It is found not in increased affluence, but in recognizing that if we have the necessities of life ('food and clothing', v. 8) we need no more. It is not abject poverty that Paul recommends, where even the necessities of life are missing; there is no blessing in that sort of deprivation. But to be satisfied with what we need, rather than always striving for the extra that we want, is the way to a contented life. Verse 7 puts our earthly ambitions in context: even the greatest of material success will last only for this life, and Paul refuses to be contained within so narrow a scope. From the perspective of eternity, it is not affluence which is gain, but godliness, and such godliness brings contentment, if only the material necessities are provided.

The root of all evil

Verse 10 is one of the most misquoted texts in the Bible. It does not say, as popular wisdom would have it, that 'money is the root of all evil'. The problem is not money itself, but the love of it, the destructive and all-consuming desire for more which Paul describes so graphically in verse 9. Such desire is the enemy of faith, and brings not contentment but misery (the 'many pains' of verse 10).

Does this sound extreme? Is it really so evil to want to enjoy the good things of life, especially as Paul has earlier opposed asceticism and recommended that we receive the gifts of God's creation with thanksgiving (4:3)? No doubt there is a balance to be struck, and it may need to be struck in different ways in different settings. But both our own happiness and our effective discipleship surely depend on giving godliness priority over material gain, and cultivating contentment rather than painfully acquiring things which one day we must leave behind.

PRAYER

Give me neither poverty nor riches;
feed me with the food that I need,
or I shall be full, and deny you, and say 'Who is the Lord?'
or I shall be poor, and steal, and profane the name of my God.

Proverbs 30:8–9

21 1 TIMOTHY 6:11–16

TAKING IT SERIOUSLY

Portrait of a 'man of God'

Paul turns with relief from the short-sighted materialism of his opponents to the qualities which are appropriate for a 'man of God' (v. 11). That striking title, which recurs in the New Testament only at 2 Timothy 3:17 (RSV), was used of great prophets and leaders of God's people in the Old Testament. Timothy is not simply one who has chosen a 'religious' career: he has been called by God and belongs to him. The qualities of 'righteousness, godliness, faith, love, endurance and gentleness' are familiar enough in the New Testament, but together they add up to a challenging and attractive portrait of the special character which God expects of those who claim to serve him.

Strenuous discipleship

Such a character does not come easily. It has to be 'pursued' (v. 11) and fought for (v. 12). It is this 'good fight', rather than the unprofitable wranglings of the false teachers (6:4–5), which must engage the energies of the man of God. In 1:18–19 we found a similar phrase, and in most English versions the translation is the same, but in fact the Greek word for 'fight' in 1:18 is a military one, whereas here (and in 2 Timothy 4:7) the word is *agonizo* (from which we get 'agonize'), a term drawn from athletics, particularly the sport of wrestling. The goal of this struggle is 'the faith', by which Paul probably means mainly the truth of the gospel for which Timothy must contend (as in 1:3–7), but the word also embraces Timothy's own life of 'faith'. That too is not to be taken for granted, and its outcome, 'eternal life', does not come by default, but has to be 'taken hold of' (v. 12), grasped, secured (the same phrase will occur in verse 19).

Paul's language here is a standing rebuke to the casual approach to Christian life and faith which is so common today. If even Timothy (and Paul himself) must bend every effort to maintain their witness and effectiveness in Christian discipleship and mission, how much more should the rest of us be on our guard against a half-hearted, slovenly, laid-back idea of what it means to be a Christian. It is not wishful thinking but constant effort which produces a 'man of God'.

The good confession

Timothy's commitment to God's service was no secret deal. The 'good confession' (v. 13) has been made before many witnesses, and such a public declaration leaves Timothy no choice over whether he should stand by his commitment, even if the going gets tough. Moreover, it is not only other people who have witnessed Timothy's stand. There are greater witnesses, no less than God 'who gives life to all things', and Jesus Christ himself. Timothy is committed to his service, and has before him the example of Jesus' own 'good confession' before Pilate. Whereas Peter crumpled before hostile witnesses, Jesus maintained his good confession unflinching, even when it took him to scourging and the cross. And that same Jesus is coming back again in glory. In the light of all this, the opposition pales into insignificance, and Timothy has no option but to continue the good fight through to the end. That is Paul's solemn charge.

God incomparable

It is typical of Paul to break off into a burst of praise (vv. 15–16), even though the letter is not yet finished (compare Romans 11:33–36; Ephesians 3:20–21). The thought of the coming 'manifestation' (v. 14) of Jesus moves him to reflect on the majesty of the one who has planned it all and will bring it about 'at the right time'. Verses 15–16 are one of the most sublime descriptions of God in the whole Bible. They call not for comment and analysis, but for meditation and for a response of praise which echoes Paul's own instinctive reaction, 'To him be honour and eternal dominion. Amen'.

FOR REFLECTION

Dwell on the words of verses 15–16. This is our God.
This is the Lord whom we are privileged to serve.
Isn't that worth a bit of 'struggle'?

22 1 TIMOTHY 6:17–21

FINAL INSTRUCTIONS

Paul returns from his 'digression' of praise to the main purpose of his letter to Timothy. In conclusion he has two sets of instructions to give, one for Timothy to pass on to others, the other for Timothy himself.

True riches

In 6:5–10 Paul issued warnings about the desire to become rich. But there are some who, by whatever means, are already rich, and it is to them that he now turns. He does not explicitly command them to 'sell all and give', as Jesus famously did to one rich young man. Rather he focuses on their attitude, both to their wealth itself and to other people who are less well off. He calls them to reassess their priorities. But we may expect that if they learn these lessons well, their generosity will make a significant hole in their accumulated wealth.

The danger of wealth is that it may encourage its possessors to worship the creature instead of the Creator. It makes people 'haughty' (v. 17), self-sufficient; by providing a hedge against disaster it can promote a sense of security and invulnerability. But such confidence is ill-founded, because wealth always remains 'uncertain'. What has been acquired can be lost, and history (both biblical and secular) is full of examples of people who wrongly thought themselves secure. There is only one sure ground for hope, and that is the God from whom all good things come, and who can be relied on to give us all we need for a good life (see comments on 6:6–8).

The other problem is in the way rich people can behave towards others. They can be materially rich but spiritually poor, since Paul understands true riches as expressed in good works and generosity (v. 18). By sharing what God has given them, they will be storing up treasure in heaven, and that treasure, unlike the slippery foundation of 'uncertain riches', will provide true security for the future. This sounds almost as if Paul believes that you can buy your way into heaven by good works of charity, but his teaching elsewhere forbids us to understand his words as crassly as that. Rather he is echoing Jesus' language about 'treasure in heaven' (Matthew 6:19–21). Such treasure is not bought, but consists of a reorientation of attitude so that we learn to put first things first. For the wealthy it means that instead of grasping for material security in the false hope that that will provide them with 'life', they are 'grasping' (the same word as in 6:12) the real life of the spirit, which is eternal.

Truth and error

'What has been entrusted to you' (v. 20), literally 'the deposit', is Paul's way of reminding Timothy of his responsible position. He has been given the true gospel and a sound grasp of Christian lifestyle and, like a banker, he must keep it safe ('guard' is again military language—he is the armed guard on duty outside the bank of faith). Other people depend on him, for his role in Ephesus is to ensure that it is this wholesome diet which is fed to the church there, and not some inferior substitute.

The alternative which is on offer is claimed by its adherents to be 'knowledge' (v. 20). The Greek word is *gnosis*, the root of the name 'Gnosticism' which describes a very widespread and insidious form of teaching which tried in the early centuries to take over the Christian Church. It was a heady amalgam of various philosophical and religious ideas which were in vogue in both pagan and Jewish circles, and which some tried to marry with the Christian gospel in a way which reminds us of the New Age movement today. But Paul is not dazzled by its intellectual and mystical attractions. For him it is all 'profane chatter and contradictions': compare his language in 1:4–7; 4:1–3; 6:3–5. And, worse, it is not only intellectually barren, but spiritually dangerous, and causes people to 'miss the mark' (v. 21). It is Timothy's job to protect the Ephesian church from this sort of dangerous nonsense, and the only way he will be able to do that is by 'guarding the deposit' of truth.

FOR REFLECTION

When the American evangelist D.L. Moody visited Britain in the nineteenth century, he was asked whether he would be doing anything for the miserably poor. 'Yes,' he said, 'and I hope also to do something for the miserably rich.'

23 2 TIMOTHY 1:1–7

TIMOTHY'S FAITH & GIFT

We do not know how much time has passed since the first letter, but the situation has changed. Paul is now again in prison (1:8, 16; 2:9) and has already been on trial (4:16). He believes that he has reached the end of his own earthly service (4:6–8). This makes Timothy's task even more important: the future of the church in Ephesus depends, humanly speaking, on him. In this second letter, then, encouragement and solemn charge are blended together with an increased sense of urgency, as Paul pulls out all the stops to strengthen the resolve of his 'beloved child' (v. 2).

Happy memories

Paul has been closely associated with Timothy ever since he 'discovered' him in Lystra some fifteen years ago (Acts 16:1–3), and has had ample opportunity to watch his spiritual progress. He is encouraged by what he has seen, and, as so often in his earlier letters to churches, begins this letter with heartfelt thanks to God.

The first ground for thanksgiving is at first sight surprising: Timothy's tears (v. 4). He is thinking, presumably, of their last parting. Clearly a close bond has developed between these two men, despite their difference in age, and in a culture which was less inhibited than ours about expressing emotion, Timothy had wept openly. Paul too has been affected by the parting, and is eager to see Timothy again. In 4:9 and 21 he will appeal to Timothy to make the journey to Rome as soon as possible, since he himself can no longer travel, and is lonely in his imprisonment. Meanwhile, he constantly remembers Timothy in his prayers. There is a depth of Christian love here which goes far beyond a 'professional' bond as fellow leaders in the Christian movement, a warmth and humanity which might surprise some whose image of Paul is as a hard-bitten intellectual and controversialist.

The second ground for thanksgiving is Timothy's faith. In one sense it is an 'inherited' faith, derived from his Jewish grandmother and mother (v. 5), who must have been among the first Christian converts on Paul's first missionary journey in Asia Minor, and from whom Timothy had learned the scriptures since childhood (3:15). People often speak of the danger of a second-hand religious experience and of the ungodly products of many a religious home. But a godly upbringing does not necessarily have this negative effect, and Paul rejoices that Timothy's faith is 'sincere'. His mother's faith has found a home (the literal meaning of 'live in', v. 5) in him as well.

The gift of leadership

As in the first letter (1 Timothy 4:14), Paul reminds Timothy of his 'ordination' (v. 6), though the more personal expression this time ('my hands', not those of the council of elders) may refer back to an earlier commissioning, perhaps when Paul first enrolled Timothy as his apostolic assistant. The gift God has given him for ministry needs to be tended. Timothy is apparently in danger, not for the first time, of giving way to his natural timidity (compare 1:8, 'do not be ashamed'; 2:1, 'be strong'), and needs to be reminded that God has called him to leadership.

The combination of 'power', 'love' and 'self-discipline' (v. 7) provides a potent recipe for Christian leadership. 'Power' alone could be too hard, 'love' alone too soft, and 'self-discipline' alone too self-centred. But when the three come together in one person, there is a leader whom others will be glad to follow, and it is such a leader that the troubled church in Ephesus needs. Timothy has been given that gift, and he must not let it die down, but rather fan it into flame.

PRAYER

We thank you, Lord, for all we have received from our families and others, but we ask that our faith may be truly our own. Whatever gifts you have given to each of us, let us not forget that we have been given them to use in your service. Amen.

24 2 TIMOTHY 1:8–12

SUFFERING *for the* GOSPEL

Shame and suffering

There seems to be good reason for the cowardice which Paul warned Timothy about in 1:7. The Christian message is not popular; it provokes hostility, and its messengers can expect to have a hard time. So it is tempting to soft-pedal at least the less appealing parts of God's message, to avoid antagonizing people. That is Timothy's danger, and Paul commands him roundly not to give way to embarrassment, either over the content of the message itself, or over the company in which it has landed him, the company of a man who is being treated like a criminal. Paul has no doubt that his imprisonment, like all his earlier apostolic suffering (catalogued in 2 Corinthians 11:23–29), is the direct result of his calling to preach the gospel.

Is it worth it?

Yes, of course, once we understand what the gospel is all about. In verses 9 and 10 a striking sequence of words and phrases spells out what is at the heart of Paul's message. It is about being 'saved', 'called with a holy calling', receiving God's 'grace'; it involves no less than the abolition of death, and the bringing to light of 'life and immortality'. This is no Sunday afternoon diversion, but a matter of life and death.

To many who heard Paul and Timothy preach, this may well have seemed extravagant language. If you think of religion as merely a matter of moral living and a set of theological beliefs, you might well be embarrassed by such a gospel, as many people still are today. But Paul's life since he met Jesus on the Damascus road has been consistently devoted to proclaiming a radical gospel of new life through the grace of God in Jesus Christ, and this note of a 'new creation' rings through all his letters (see, for example, 2 Corinthians 4:6; 5:17). In comparison with that gospel, as he declares so eloquently in Philippians 3:4–14, nothing else matters, and if his calling to proclaim that gospel leads him into suffering, imprisonment and even death, that is not too high a price to pay. After all, in 'the appearing of our Saviour Christ Jesus' (v. 10), death (*real* death) has been abolished, and a

Roman sentence of execution is only the means to the experience of the 'life and immortality' which is the very object of his gospel message.

Nor is this revolutionary message something newly coined by Paul. It is the culmination of God's purpose determined 'before the ages began' (v. 9). The coming of Jesus was no divine afterthought. But it is the amazing privilege of Paul and Timothy to be there at the time when what has so long been in preparation is now at last openly revealed, and to be entrusted with the task of telling everybody about it. Now *that* is worth suffering for!

Safe in God's hands

It is God who has saved and called us, and so when suffering comes we may rely on his power to carry us through (v. 8). What is put in his hands will be safe to the end (v. 12). The Greek phrase at the end of verse 12 is simply 'my deposit', and this can be translated either 'what I have entrusted to him' or 'what he has entrusted to me'. The English versions vary over which they choose, but I doubt if Paul would have been too worried, because both are obviously appropriate senses. Paul has entrusted himself to God, and God will keep him safe. And God has entrusted to Paul a message and a ministry, and he may be relied on to look after him as he fulfils it.

So in the end, despite all Paul's urgent appeals to Timothy to rekindle his gift and stand firm in his faith and teaching, the success of the mission is assured because it is not ultimately in the hands of Timothy or Paul, but of the God whose gospel they have been called to preach and whose salvation they have already tasted and may confidently look forward to experiencing right through to the end.

In the light of that confidence, what room is there for shame, and what does present suffering matter?

PRAYER

Lord, help us to grasp the truth and the glory of the gospel as firmly as Paul did, so that we may also share his confidence, and know ourselves to be safe in your hands. Amen.

25 2 TIMOTHY 1:13–18

DESERTERS & *a* GOOD FRIEND

Guarding the treasure

Verses 13–14 sum up Timothy's responsibility. The 'sound teaching' which he has received from Paul (the gospel which we have just read about in 1:9–10) is a real treasure. It is a message about 'faith and love', and it will be by modelling those essential Christian qualities that Timothy will commend the gospel to others and keep the treasure safe for those who need to discover it for themselves.

When Timothy received this teaching from Paul, and when he was placed in Ephesus to teach and defend it, he was given a trusted commission (the same Greek word, 'deposit', as we met in 1:12). With Paul far away in prison, it may seem a lonely task, but as he stands guard he is not alone, for he has the presence of the Holy Spirit 'living in us'. This remarkable language occurs also in Romans 8:11, where Paul similarly explains how a successful Christian life depends not only on us (if it did, there would be little hope!) but on the presence of the Holy Spirit in our lives. God is not only *with* the believer, but *in* us by the Holy Spirit. What more could we need?

Disappointment and encouragement

In verses 15–18 we read of two contrasting attitudes to Paul and his ministry on the part of his former friends in Asia (of which Ephesus was the capital).

On the one hand, there has been a large-scale desertion: 'all who are in Asia' (v. 15), even if a little exaggerated, sounds pretty comprehensive! Presumably Paul is talking about what has happened since he himself was in Ephesus, and in the light of the language about shame in 1:8 and 16 it seems likely that Paul's imprisonment has led many to want to dissociate themselves from him. If so many have turned against Paul, it is no wonder that he is so concerned for Timothy, who is now his representative in what must be becoming an increasingly hostile environment. In repudiating Paul, they have also presumably turned against his message, and the whole integrity of the Christian movement in Ephesus seems to be under threat. We know nothing else about Phygelus and Hermogenes, but it sounds as if they were former friends and associates of Paul, and he is distressed to hear of their disloyalty.

But fortunately that is not the whole story about the church in Ephesus. There is also Onesiphorus, whose loyalty stands out the more clearly in contrast with the deserters. It seems that he comes from Ephesus (where he has already rendered good service to the cause of the gospel, v. 18), but has found his way to Rome, and has made a point of seeking out Paul in his imprisonment. Probably he has given such practical help as was possible in the circumstances (the sort of help Paul asks Timothy to give in 4:13). Certainly his moral support has been a vital help in Paul's loneliness and discouragement.

We know no more about Onesiphorus. It is curious that Paul asks for God's mercy on his *household* (v. 16), and many have concluded that Onesiphorus must have recently died, leaving a bereaved family in Ephesus—though it is also possible that Paul mentions the household because he is aware that while Onesiphorus has been with him in Rome, the rest of his family in Ephesus has stood out against the general desertion, and has remained loyal in support of Paul and his gospel. We simply do not know what the situation was, but perhaps Paul's wish that Onesiphorus may find mercy 'on that day' (presumably the day of judgment) favours the likelihood that he has died. In that case it seems that Onesiphorus, like Paul himself, has finished his race with honour, and can look forward to the 'crown of righteousness' which God will award 'on that day' (4:7–8).

PRAYER

Lord, may I be an Onesiphorus, and not a Phygelus or Hermogenes! Amen.

26 2 TIMOTHY 2:1–7

NO GAINS WITHOUT PAINS

The apostolic succession

Paul's work is finished, and Timothy has now taken up the apostolic baton. But that is not to be the end of the matter, and in verse 2 Paul sets out a central principle of leadership which the Church ignores at its peril. No Christian generation dare care only for its own health and growth; each must make provision for the generations to follow.

So Timothy's task is not limited only to his own teaching, crucial as that must be in the current volatile situation. He must also be looking out for the teachers of the future. And those teachers are to be selected not only for their own ability to teach, but for their capacity to inspire and equip a further generation of teachers. So the apostolic succession must continue, from Paul to Timothy, from Timothy to his 'faithful people', from those faithful people to others, and so on into centuries to come. Its history has not been an untroubled one, and there have been times when the succession has appeared to be lost, and the gospel has had to be rediscovered by going back to the original apostolic writings. But Paul and Timothy and their successors did their job well, and we today are heirs to that same gospel tradition. Now it is for us too to make sure that it remains in the hands of 'faithful people who will be able to teach others as well'.

Success does not come cheap

The theme of suffering is seldom far away in this letter. That is why Timothy must again be urged to 'be strong' (v. 1), and to take his share of suffering as Christ's soldier. We noted in 1 Timothy 6:12 that the metaphor of 'fighting' there was, in fact, drawn from athletics rather than from warfare, but here (as in 1 Timothy 1:18) the language is unambiguously military. Modern hymn books tend to edit out the military metaphors of our forebears, but Paul has no such inhibitions. To be in Christian service is to be enrolled in an army, with all the hardship which that inevitably involves.

He spells it out by means of three parallel illustrations in verses 4–6. The first is again that of the soldier, whose aim is not his own pleasure but 'to please the enlisting officer'. In other words, he is under orders, and any other considerations must take second place to being a good soldier. Civilian pursuits must be set aside for as long as he is in the army—and the Christian army is an enrolment for life. We cannot afford to get 'entangled' with lesser concerns.

Then Paul turns again to athletics, but this time his focus is not so much on the physical demands of athletics, but on the element of discipline. Those who run and jump for fun are not likely to reach the record books. There is the discipline of constant training, and there is the discipline of the rule-book. If you are a serious athlete and want to win, you cannot compete just when you feel like it, or make up your own rules.

Thirdly, there is sheer hard work, illustrated by the farmer. Many who have been attracted by the rural idyll have quickly discovered that agricultural success does not just fall into your lap. You have to work for it.

All this sounds rather grim and forbidding. Is there no enjoyment in the Christian life, no fun in serving God? It must be admitted that 'fun' is not the first word that comes to mind when we think of Paul's life and letters. He was single-minded and pushed himself very hard. Of course there is a softer side to discipleship, but Paul warns Timothy and us against allowing that softer element to have the upper hand. Worthwhile achievements do not come from self-indulgence.

Verse 7 then comes as a challenge to us as well, to ponder Paul's uncompromising illustrations of what is involved in being a faithful disciple. As they say in Yorkshire, 'Think on!'

FOR REFLECTION

What other illustrations from modern life might we add to the soldier, the athlete and the farmer? Can you think of examples of people whose Christian lives and ministry illustrate the value of discipline—or of people who illustrate the opposite?

27 2 TIMOTHY 2:8–13

FAITHFULNESS—OURS & GOD'S

Paul the good soldier

In verses 8–10 Paul continues his encouragement to Timothy to hold fast, now by reminding him of his own example. His imprisonment is only the culmination of a lifetime of suffering which has come as a result of his apostolic ministry. It makes him seem like a criminal (hence the fear that his fellow Christians might be ashamed to be associated with him, 1:8, 16). But even that has to be endured 'for the sake of the elect' (v. 10).

We do not know the charge on which Paul has been imprisoned at this time, but he seems convinced that it is his faithfulness to the gospel which has put him there. If imprisonment is the price of maintaining the gospel without compromise, he is content to be treated like a criminal. But how does it help the cause of the gospel to have its chief preacher locked up? For all Paul's sense of the importance of his apostolic commission, he is far from thinking of himself as personally indispensable to God. It is the word of God, not its messenger, which carries the power of salvation, and that word remains free. Timothy and others can carry on where Paul has left off, and so the gospel will continue to spread and to bring salvation.

For the gospel is not the gospel of Paul, but the gospel of Jesus Christ. The very basic summary of the gospel in verse 8 is strikingly similar to the summary at the beginning of Paul's letter to the Romans (Romans 1:3–4), with the same two key elements of Jesus' descent from David and his resurrection. The stress on the resurrection does not surprise us: it is at the heart of the New Testament proclamation. But the descent from David, affirming Jesus' status as the Jewish Messiah, may seem to us less central. But Paul was a Jew, who had himself at first opposed this 'upstart' Messiah. So his teaching, especially to his fellow Jews, must begin at the beginning. It does no harm for us too to be reminded of the concrete historical context in which the gospel came to us, not through an angelic message but in the life, death and resurrection of a Jewish man.

A 'poem' with a twist in the tail

The thought of the 'eternal glory' which is the goal of the gospel (v. 10) causes Paul to launch into what sounds like a poem (vv. 11–13), perhaps a verse of a hymn, perhaps his own way of putting his thoughts about God's faithfulness into a memorable form for teaching. The 'poem' has four balancing lines, but in the fourth line it seems to go wrong—and in that 'going wrong' is the heart of its message!

The first two lines pose no problems for our understanding. They assure us that those who suffer with and for Christ, even to the point of death, can look forward with confidence to life and glory. Here is the familiar Pauline theme of sharing in the experiences of Christ, which is spelled out more fully in such passages as Romans 6:3–11 and Ephesians 2:4–6.

The second pair of lines is different. It begins in the third line with a warning that to deny Christ is to risk being repudiated by him (compare Jesus' words in Mark 8:38). That is what strict justice demands. And so in the fourth line we expect, 'If we are faithless, he will be faithless too'. But Paul cannot say that! The cold logic of the 'poem' has to give way to the glorious *non sequitur* of verse 13, because God is *God*: faithfulness, as we might say, is his middle name. If he were to abandon us, even when we have proved faithless, he would not only be denying us, but denying *himself*. Throughout the Old Testament God has revealed himself as a God of 'steadfast love', who delights to call his people back when they have let him down, and to keep his side of the covenant even when his people abandon theirs.

So retributive logic gives way before divine grace. It may be theologically untidy, but isn't it gloriously true?

PRAYER

Thank you, Lord, that you do not deal with us as we deserve.
Help us to share that good news with those around us
who need to hear it. Amen.

28 2 TIMOTHY 2:14–19

The POWER *of a* WORD

Timothy's task in Ephesus is all about words. He is, above all, a teacher, charged with 'reminding' and 'warning' (v. 14) the Christians about what their commitment to Jesus involves. In these verses we see both the danger of words wrongly used, and the importance of using the 'word of truth' responsibly.

Unhelpful words

We have already seen several times how concerned Paul is about some currents of teaching which are becoming popular in Ephesus, and which he believes have the potential to undermine the 'sound teaching' of the gospel. Here he uses several expressions, which probably all have as their target the same people, but which give us different facets of his concern.

'Wrangling over words' recalls the 'morbid craving for controversy and disputes about words' in 1 Timothy 6:4 (compare 1 Timothy 1:3–7; 4:1–3; 6:20). Probably it is the same 'Gnostic'-type speculations which have continued to fascinate some of the Ephesian church members, and have made them increasingly argumentative. The result is not enlightenment but ruin for the hearers. The gospel promotes good living, but these heady ideas produce only argument. It is all 'profane chatter' (v. 16), and its result is increased impiety rather than growth in godliness.

Yet people seem unable to see how dangerous such teaching is. It appeals to their intellectual pride, and so spreads 'like gangrene' (v. 17). If it were just harmless chatter it might be overlooked as merely silly, but it has gone far beyond that, to the point where some people's Christian commitment is in doubt: they are 'upsetting the faith of some' (v. 18). In particular, the idea is getting around that 'the resurrection has already taken place'.

The reference is not, of course, to the resurrection of Jesus—that had indeed already taken place, and was the very foundation of the gospel. But Jesus' resurrection carried also the promise of new life for those who believe in him, and Paul's teaching has focused strongly on this element of looking forward. Romans 8:18–30 is a powerful statement of the future hope which is at the heart of Christian faith.

But the point of that passage is that it remains a *hope* as long as we continue in this life. Yet it seems that some people in Ephesus were not prepared to live in hope, and were claiming that they were already living the resurrection life, that it was possible to have it all now. (Compare the people at Thessalonica who thought the second coming of Jesus had already taken place: 2 Thessalonians 2:2.)

Faced with such unsettling teaching, Paul is not afraid to name names (as also in 1:15 and 4:14). Hymenaeus (v. 17) has the dubious distinction of already having been named (along with Alexander who will reappear in 4:14) as a dangerous teacher in 1 Timothy 1:19–20. It seems that Paul's attempt there to 'excommunicate' him has not solved the problem. Clearly Paul expects Timothy to be no less forthright in confronting error.

The word of truth

Bad words must be confronted with good. Verse 15 sets out Timothy's responsibility as that of a workman who has to satisfy his employer (God). The material he is working with is 'the word of truth', the gospel entrusted to him by Paul (and ultimately by God), and his job is, literally, to 'cut it straight'. The picture may be that of a ploughman cutting a straight furrow, or of a carpenter or mason fashioning his material truly. The metaphor implies that he is responsible not only to repeat what he has been told, but to work with it, presumably by explaining and applying the sound teaching of the gospel for the benefit and spiritual growth of those he has been called to lead. Only so will he be able to counteract the pernicious influence of people like Hymenaeus.

FOR REFLECTION

Verse 19 speaks of two 'inscriptions' on God's foundation stone: 'The Lord knows those who are his' and 'Let everyone who calls on the name of the Lord turn away from wickedness'. How do you think the double 'inscription' relates to the respective situations of Hymenaeus and Timothy? Can you think of areas of teaching current today which need to be confronted with the 'word of truth'? How should that word be 'cut straight' in your situation?

29 2 TIMOTHY 2:20–26

The LORD'S SERVANT

Ready for service

All the utensils in the Lord's house are useful (v. 20). But while all members of the church are needed, some have a special role, and Paul clearly thinks it is appropriate to want to be available for more special service, to be utensils of silver or gold. Not only Timothy himself, but other church members, are encouraged to make themselves 'ready for every good work' (v. 21). There are both negative and positive ways to do so.

Negatively, there are things to be 'cleansed from' (v. 21). At this point he does not spell out what they are, but in the light of all that has already been said about dangerous and unhelpful tendencies in the church, there is no doubt what he means. In verses 22 and 23 he is more specific. Verse 23 covers familiar ground—the arguments and quarrels which are dividing and weakening the church. Anyone who aspires to be a useful utensil must keep clear of such folly. But what are the 'youthful passions' which must also be shunned (v. 22)? People often think Paul is talking specifically about sexual temptation, but the context does not indicate that. Rather, the 'youthful passions' are to be defined by contrast with their opposites which he spells out in the rest of this verse. It is the headstrong arrogance of youth which militates against these godly qualities, and leads people into destructive arguments in the search for novelty and the desire to impress.

By contrast, the good qualities listed in verse 22 speak for themselves. They are the qualities that make for good relationships and spiritual growth. They reflect the character of God himself, and they grow naturally in 'those who call on the Lord from a pure heart'. It is by cultivating these qualities that a person will be 'ready for every good work', a utensil of gold.

Blessed are the peacemakers

The Authorized Version translates verse 24 by 'The servant of the Lord must not *strive*', and that has sometimes been taken as a prescription for laid-back discipleship, an excuse for taking the easy way. Nothing could be further from the truth. The literal translation is 'must not *fight*': it is a warning against being quarrelsome and confrontational in Timothy's dealings with members of the church. Rather than responding in kind to the quarrelsomeness of people like Hymenaeus, he is to be positive, constructive, aiming for peace rather than division—and that is certainly not the easy or the natural way.

Peace is not to be sought at the expense of truth. The kindness, gentleness and patience prescribed in verses 24–25 are the qualities of an understanding teacher. The phrase 'an apt teacher' is not an incongruous insertion into a list of attractive character traits, but focuses what is the object of the whole description of the Lord's servant. Surrounded by quarrelsome opponents, he is to show the opposite qualities and, by so doing, if possible, to win them to a better frame of mind. So opponents are not to be tolerated or ignored. They are to be 'corrected', but the way to do this is by kindness.

The ideas, and the attitudes, of Timothy's opponents come not from God but from the devil. They are under his power, and so are promoting his cause. That is why it is so important that Timothy does not simply fight back with the same weapons. The object of his patient and sensitive teaching is to win them back, and for that purpose it is the weapons of love which will prevail. Behind all the human argument in the Ephesian church is a supernatural conflict; if the opponents are to be restored to a better way, it must be by God's means, and in the end it will be the work not of Timothy but of the God whom he serves.

PRAYER

Lord, help us to reflect your own character of love, peace and purity. Make us gentle and understanding. Guard us from quarrelsomeness, and use us to promote the cause of peace and truth in your church. Amen.

30 2 TIMOTHY 3:1–9

Testing Times

For all his praise of peace and gentleness, Paul does not pull his punches when it comes to describing those whom he regards as a danger to the church. His mention in 2:26 of the devil's hand in all this now leads him into one of his most lurid diatribes.

'In the last days'

This phrase (v. 1) might suggest that Paul is here looking into the distant future. But it is the consistent message of the New Testament that, with the coming of Jesus, the 'last days' to which the Old Testament prophets looked forward have already been inaugurated. Paul and his contemporaries were conscious of already living in the last days. And it is clear from the way these verses are expressed that they describe not some far-off time of distress, but the very situation with which Timothy is now involved in Ephesus. In the extravagant and dangerous teaching and actions of these people, Paul sees the culmination of the opposition to God and his people which has been a feature of the world ever since Jannes and Jambres (v. 8, the traditional Jewish names for the Egyptian magicians described in Exodus 7:11–12, 22; 8:7) stood up against Moses and Aaron and attempted to thwart the purpose of the one true God.

A rogues' gallery

The list of vices in verses 2–5 is the sort of thing we find in many polemical documents from the ancient (and indeed the modern) world. It does not reach the heights of abuse found in 2 Peter 2 and the letter of Jude, but it is bad enough. It is probably not profitable to dwell on the vices listed one by one—their effect is in their cumulative force. But one or two comments may be in order.

The first phrase, 'lovers of themselves' (v. 2), sums up the thrust of much of the list. These are people who cannot or will not see things from the other person's point of view, whose every effort is bent on their own self-advancement and on using other people to their own advantage. As such, the list is in complete and depressing contrast with the qualities of the 'Lord's servant' in 2:24–25.

The end of the list adds a further dimension to this catalogue of self-centredness. These people not only have no time for anyone else, but also they have no time for God. It is 'pleasure' (v. 4), not God, that has their allegiance. Yet Paul is clearly not talking about people outside the Christian (or at least religious) community, since they maintain 'the outward form of godliness' (v. 5). Remember what Jesus said about 'wolves in sheep's clothing' (Matthew 7:15)? They use the right language, and may seem very plausible to other people in the church. But it is all on the surface: there is no 'power' to it. So Timothy must not be taken in, but rather 'avoid them' (v. 5), in case he too might be infected with their religious hypocrisy.

People at risk

Where there are rogues, there are also too often gullible people for them to take advantage of (vv. 6–7). The word translated 'silly women' is a diminutive ('little women'), used not for women in general but for the type of vulnerable women who are easy prey for plausible peddlers of religious novelties. Paul describes them as morbidly burdened by a sense of guilt and eager for new spiritual nostrums—religious dilettantes, always searching but never finding. It is a fair question whether that sort of character is found only among women, but clearly at Ephesus this was where these teachers with a veneer of religious language ('counterfeit faith', v. 8) were finding easy pickings. In the light of the success which they seem to have been enjoying, it is remarkable and reassuring that Paul can so confidently look forward to the ultimate triumph of truth over error (v. 9).

FOR REFLECTION

'Always being instructed, but never able to arrive at a knowledge of the truth' (v. 7): can you recognize this as a description of some people's approach to religion today? What is to be done about it?

31 2 TIMOTHY 3:10–13

The MARKS *of an* APOSTLE

The letter continues to shift the spotlight between the false teachers and the true servants of God. In contrast to the lurid portrait of the opponents in 3:1–9, Paul reminds Timothy of his own example. Indeed no one should know it better than Timothy, since as Paul's closest companion he has had ample opportunity to observe his life-style. The verb translated 'observe' (v. 10) is more literally to 'follow' or 'accompany', and was used especially of the disciples of a religious or philosophical teacher, who by keeping close to their master learned to imitate his life as well as his teaching.

Apostolic lifestyle

The list of qualities to be imitated in verse 10 contrasts powerfully with the list of vices in 3:2–5. Paul has nothing to be ashamed of, either in what he has done or in the reasons for which he has done it, and Timothy may safely take him as a role model. The first three features ('teaching', 'conduct', 'aim in life') sum up Paul's ministry. His actions have been consistent with his words, and both have been directed by a clear sense of purpose, ever since God called him to proclaim the gospel to the nations. Then follow four qualities ('faith', 'patience', 'love', 'steadfastness') which sum up the sort of man he has been, the character traits which have motivated and sustained his life and ministry for so many years. Most of us would shrink from such self-advertisement, and would consider it immodest. But Paul has no time for false modesty. If these claims are true, they are testimony to the grace of God in his life, and to draw attention to them (in contrast with the way some people in the church at Ephesus are behaving) is an essential part of his contribution as an apostolic model.

Apostolic suffering

The mention of 'steadfastness' leads Paul on to speak of what he has had to undergo in his apostolic ministry. Timothy knows these too from personal observation, for it was during Paul's first visit to Antioch, Iconium and Lystra that Timothy first heard the gospel of Jesus Christ. It was a time of powerful evangelism, but as so often in Paul's experience, the progress of the gospel was accompanied by violent opposition, culminating in Paul's being left for dead outside Timothy's home town of Lystra. (See Acts 13:44—14:20 for the events in the three cities.)

You would think it would have been enough to put Timothy off getting involved with this unpopular new movement, but Paul seems to be able to take such experience in his stride as an occupational hazard. Indeed, verse 12 goes further and takes it for granted that not only pioneer missionaries but also 'all who want to live a godly life in Christ Jesus' must expect such treatment. Just as Jesus had warned his disciples that the world which rejected him would reject them as well (John 15:18–25; compare Matthew 5:11–12), so Paul also assumes that to follow Jesus faithfully is the way to unpopularity and persecution. There is too much at stake in the gospel message—those who cannot love it will loathe it, and will react with hostility to those who continue to confront them with the challenge of a godly life.

This is not just a temporary problem: Paul expects the opposition to go from bad to worse (v. 13). But the last word is not with those who reject the gospel, but with God, who has rescued Paul out of all his suffering so far (v. 11), and who Paul is sure will continue to do so (4:17–18). In throwing in his lot with Paul, Timothy has certainly not opted for an easy life, but he may be assured that God will not let him down, and steadfastness like that of Paul will be rewarded.

FOR REFLECTION

Does your experience tally with Paul's words in verse 12? What should be the Christian response to opposition and persecution?

32 2 TIMOTHY 3:14–17

The VALUE *of* SCRIPTURE

Timothy's heritage

From his Jewish mother and grandmother (1:5; Acts 16:1) Timothy has received a thorough grounding in the Old Testament. The 'sacred writings' and 'scripture' referred to in this passage must mean the Old Testament, since the books which now make up our New Testament had not yet been brought together into a 'Bible'; indeed some of them had not yet been written. Besides, it was from childhood that Timothy had known these sacred writings, long before Paul and the Christian gospel came on the scene. Now that the fuller light of the gospel has come, there is no suggestion that the existing scriptures have become out of date. Far from it. Timothy must continue in what he has learned and believed, and that includes what he learned as a half-Jewish boy from his mother. (Note that 'from whom you learned it' in verse 14 is in the plural: this is not just what Paul has taught him.)

'Inspired by God'

To call scripture 'inspired' (v. 16) is a statement not about its literary quality but about its origin. The single word translated 'inspired by God' means literally 'God-breathed'. While Paul was well aware of the various human authors through whom the 'sacred writings' had come to be written, he looks beyond their human authorship to their ultimate source. They come from God. That is what it means to single out these writings (for there were plenty of other good books available) as 'sacred' and as 'scripture'. In reading these words penned by historical Israelites, we are also reading the 'word of God'.

The Old Testament and the gospel

These ancient Hebrew writings, which some people today think we may safely leave on one side now that we have the directly Christian witness of the New Testament, are in fact 'able to instruct you for salvation through faith in Christ Jesus' (v. 15). The coming of Jesus was the fulfilment of the hope of the Old Testament writers, and the salvation made available through him is the culmination of God's purpose of blessing for his people. The Old Testament, even on its own, points forward to the Christian gospel. Read now in the light of that gospel, it is full of Jesus.

How scripture works

The four nouns which conclude verse 16 sum up the function of scripture as the word of God. It 'teaches' by informing us of the truth about God and his relation with his people. It 'reproves' by showing us where we are failing to live and think as the people of God. It 'corrects' by guiding us instead into right behaviour and thinking. And it 'trains in righteousness' by spelling out the will of God and by challenging us to follow it. These four components in the 'usefulness' of scripture warn us against any purely intellectual interest in the Bible. It does indeed 'teach', and that teaching is the essential foundation of all that follows; but if the result of that teaching does not affect also the way we live, it has not fulfilled its purpose.

The object of the exercise

Our study of the sacred writings, if it is effective, should have a practical outcome. It may sometimes provide us with quite specific guidance for our discipleship but, more fundamentally than that, it should also be steadily building up our spiritual life and maturity. The object is that all who belong to God may become 'proficient' (v. 17: the word implies 'fully prepared') so as to be able to live as God requires. Paul seems to have in mind not only a set of rules and regulations to follow, but a 'Christian mind' such as will enable us to make right decisions when faced with hard choices. For such a 'proficiency' there is no substitute for long and careful exposure to the sacred writings. If Timothy should expect to find the Old Testament 'useful' for this purpose, how much more should we, who have the New as well!

PRAYER

Blessed Lord, who hast caused all Holy Scriptures to be written for our learning, grant that we may in such wise hear them, read, mark, learn and inwardly digest them, that by patience and comfort of thy holy word we may embrace and ever hold fast that hope of everlasting life which thou hast given us in thy Son, our Saviour Jesus Christ. Amen.

Book of Common Prayer

33 2 TIMOTHY 4:1–5

A Solemn Charge

As Paul prepares to hand over the baton (4:6–8), he sums up his instructions to Timothy in this resounding final charge. And it is not just Paul's personal direction, but is uttered 'in the presence of God and of Christ Jesus' (v. 1), not merely as witnesses to the charge, but in the light of the ultimate judgment of Christ when he will appear as king, when Timothy must give account of his stewardship. This is really serious.

Itching ears

The charge focuses on the ministry of proclaiming 'sound doctrine' (vv. 3–4). The word translated 'sound' is more literally 'healthy' or, as we might say, 'wholesome'. Paul uses this word a lot in these letters (1 Timothy 1:10; 6:3; 2 Timothy 1:13; 4:3; Titus 1:9, 13; 2:1, 2). The health of the churches is threatened by wrong teaching, and Paul is acutely aware of that threat in both Ephesus and Crete. He has spoken several times of the currents of silly and dangerous ideas that are around (2:16–18; 3:1–9, 13). Not only are such notions wrong in themselves, but they blunt people's appetite for the truth. People who follow such teaching become spiritual dilettanti; novelty becomes more important than truth, and the result is a titillating, make-believe world of myths. Do we find it very difficult to recognize the same tendency in some of the so-called spirituality of our day, particularly in the weird mix of ideas which we call New Age?

Preach the word

Timothy's role as guardian of the truth of the apostolic gospel is clear—he must proclaim it (v. 2). And that proclamation is not reserved to 11 o'clock on Sunday morning. As someone has said, there are only two times when we should preach the gospel: in season, and out of season! When it suits and when it doesn't. Does he refer only to the convenience or inconvenience of the preacher? Or is he also saying that people must be confronted with the truth even when it doesn't suit *them*? That way lies fanaticism and unpopularity, but Paul never seems to have shrunk from either, if the ministry of the gospel demanded it.

Nor is it just a matter of 'proclamation' in the sense of a message delivered with a take-it-or-leave-it indifference. 'Convince, rebuke, encourage' is the language of close personal involvement, applying the message directly to the people and looking for a response. The preacher is also the pastor, who cares for the flock individually and works to keep each one in the way of 'healthy' thinking and living. And that takes time and tireless effort, 'the utmost patience in teaching'. Such a ministry is demanding and uncomfortable. No wonder Timothy needs such a solemn charge.

The work of an evangelist

Timothy is not primarily an 'evangelist' (v. 5) in the sense of a pioneer preacher of the gospel. It is his role to consolidate and develop the work after Paul the pioneer has moved on. But he is none the less there as a champion of the good news, and as such he remains an 'evangelist'; indeed, his situation puts a strong question mark against those who would separate the work of a pastor from that of an evangelist. The ministry he is called on to 'fulfil' or 'make the most of' is that of a gospel-man in all its aspects. And that work demands all his resources and concentration. 'Be sober' no doubt includes avoiding literal drunkenness, but it is wider than that. His life must be free of distraction, free to focus clearly on his vital work. It will not be easy: suffering is apparently an inseparable part of his ministry. For Paul, and therefore for Timothy, the work of the gospel is an all-or-nothing commitment; it is too important for anything less.

FOR REFLECTION

How far is Paul's charge to Timothy appropriate only to his specific responsibility as leader of the difficult church in Ephesus, and how far would he say the same to any and all of us in our different situations? Is the ministry of the gospel always such a demanding business?

34 2 TIMOTHY 4:6–8

'I HAVE FINISHED *the* RACE'

Paul is about to die. Perhaps he has received a clear message from God to that effect (just as earlier he had been told that he would be spared to complete his work in Corinth, Acts 18:9–10). But in any case his circumstances in prison in Rome now leave little room for doubt. He is, in effect, already on 'death row' (v. 6). His confidence in God's presence and support is no less (4:17–18), but now he knows that it is not God's purpose to keep him at his earthly ministry. It is time to move on. These verses therefore give us an important insight into how a great Christian leader thinks about death. The contrast with the way most people think could hardly be greater.

An offering to God

A libation (v. 6) was a familiar part of Greek religion, a cup of wine poured out as an offering to the gods. But the Old Testament also provided for drink-offerings to be added to an animal sacrifice (Numbers 15:5–10), and this is more likely what Paul had in mind, as in Philippians 2:17–18 where he pictures himself being 'poured out as a libation over the sacrifice and the offering of your faith'. So his death is to be no accident, but a sacrificial offering to God. Just as his life has been lived for God, so his death will also be for God. It will be the culmination of his service.

Looking back

Verse 7 sounds almost smug, and perhaps it is not easy to draw the line between complacent self-congratulation and a justified satisfaction in a job well done. But if anyone had a right to look back with satisfaction, surely it was Paul, one of history's greatest achievers. He speaks in the first person singular: '*I* have fought, finished, kept'; yet Paul would have been the first to add 'Yet not I, but the grace of God that is with me' (1 Corinthians 15:10).

He has used the imagery of the wrestling match before: see comments on 1 Timothy 6:12. Here the same athletic imagery is used: Paul sees his life and ministry as a wrestling bout, in which he has fought through to the end. Similarly, it has been a long-distance race, and he has finished the course. He does not speak of having *won* either the wrestling bout or the race, but simply of having stuck it out to the end. History would judge that in fact Paul *had* won, in that the gospel he so energetically proclaimed and defended would in due course conquer the Roman Empire itself and become the greatest religious force in the world. But all that was hidden from Paul. It was enough for him that he had fulfilled his task. The rest was in God's hands.

So he does not speak of his having won converts and established churches, but simply of having himself 'kept the faith'. Despite all the suffering and abuse, he has remained true to his trust, and now he can turn in his account to God with no cause for shame or regret.

Now it is for Timothy to take up the baton.

Looking forward

Someone once described death to me as 'promotion'. I think Paul would have agreed.

The 'crown' he speaks of (v. 8) is the wreath awarded to a successful competitor in the games. But Paul does not think of this as a personal honour to him as an individual *victor ludorum*. Rather it is for all who have stayed the course, whom Paul describes simply as those who have 'longed for his (Christ's) appearing'. The Christian race is not competitive. It is one in which, as the Dodo says in *Alice in Wonderland*, 'Everybody has won and all must have prizes.'

As the judge who will award the wreath is 'righteous', so that wreath is of 'righteousness'. The Greek word means not only 'behaving right', but also, and especially in Paul, 'being right with God', so that it means much the same as 'salvation'. This is the ultimate *shalom* (peace, well-being), compared to which all earthly joy is only a weak foreshadowing.

FOR REFLECTION

Fight the good fight with all thy might;
Christ is thy strength, and Christ thy right.
Lay hold on life, and it shall be
Thy joy and crown eternally.

J.S.B. Monsell (1811–75)

35 2 TIMOTHY 4:9–15

PERSONAL MESSAGES

After the grand scale of the language in the last section, these verses remind us that this is, after all, a personal letter to a friend and colleague. From Paul the noble spiritual athlete, we turn to Paul the prisoner, cold and lonely, and let down by those who should have been at his side. He wants Timothy to be with him in his distress.

A roll-call of Paul's colleagues

Quite frequently in Paul's letters and in Acts, we read of people who worked with Paul in his apostolic ministry to the churches of Asia and Europe. Of the six men mentioned in verses 10–12, all except Crescens have appeared elsewhere as part of Paul's circle of associates, but now, with Paul in prison in Rome, the band is scattered, and 'only Luke is with me' (v. 11).

In happier days, Demas (v. 10) was associated with Luke as one of Paul's fellow workers in Asia Minor (Colossians 4:14; Philemon 24). Now Paul sees him as a deserter. His 'love for the present world' contrasts sharply with the 'love of Christ's appearing' which Paul has singled out as the mark of true believers in verse 8. We have no means of knowing whether Paul means by this that Demas has abandoned his Christian profession altogether, or simply that he attributes his move to Thessalonica, leaving Paul in prison, to an unworthily selfish motive.

Tychicus, on the other hand (v. 12), has gone away at Paul's request, probably in order to carry this letter to Timothy at Ephesus (his own home church). Nothing is said of why Crescens and Titus (v. 10) have moved away, but the fact that they are linked so closely with Demas (the same verb covers them all in Greek) may indicate that they too, unlike Tychicus, went without Paul's approval. If, as most people think, this is the same Titus, and this letter was written after the letter to Titus, this might mark an unhappy development in what had been a relationship of trust between Paul and Titus, one of his most long-standing colleagues. But we must be careful of arguing too much from silence.

At any rate, Paul has none of his colleagues left with him except the faithful Luke, his companion on many of his earlier journeys and while he was imprisoned in Caesarea (see the passages in Acts where Luke writes in the first person, 'we'). Perhaps, as Paul's 'beloved physician' (Colossians 4:14), he had a specially important role while Paul endured his last imprisonment. But Paul is lonely, and longs for the company of Timothy, and also of Mark, another of the core group who were with him when he wrote Colossians (Colossians 4:10). It is especially heartening to hear of Paul's desire for Mark's company, and his description of him as 'useful in my ministry' (v. 11), when we recall that this was the man whom Paul had once refused to take as a travelling companion, and had apparently written off as a failure (Acts 15:36–40). Failure in God's service need not be permanent, and Paul was a wise enough pastor to revise his opinion of Mark in the light of experience.

Instructions for Timothy

Verse 13 is delightfully trivial, and yet reveals something of the real Paul, expecting to be cold in prison as winter came on (4:21) and so needing his cloak—and also short of reading matter! The 'books' were scrolls, but we cannot know whether they were scriptural texts or other documents. Those made of 'parchment' (animal skin) would be more important documents than the more everyday texts which were usually written on papyrus.

The other instruction is quite different, and recalls earlier warnings in these letters against specific individuals (1 Timothy 1:20; 2 Timothy 1:15; 2:17). We do not know specifically what harm Alexander has done to Paul; nor can we be sure, since the name was a common one, whether this is the same man as we met in 1 Timothy 1:20. If he is, then as a former member of the church his 'strong opposition' (v. 15) to the gospel would be particularly damaging. Timothy, it seems, is surrounded by dangerous and influential people. He cannot afford to relax his guard.

Contrast Paul's comment that 'the Lord will pay him back' (v. 14) with his prayer in 4:16; see Romans 12:19 for Paul's attitude to retribution.

PRAYER

Thank you, Lord, for companions and helpers in our Christian lives and ministry. Help us in our turn to be faithful friends and loyal colleagues, and help us also to know whom we can trust. Amen.

36 2 TIMOTHY 4:16–22

PAUL *on* TRIAL

The 'first defence'

Paul's brief comments on his situation in verses 16–18 leave us unclear about just what has happened. The reference to a 'first defence' suggests that at the time of writing the trial is not yet finished, and that Paul faces a further hearing (and one which he has little doubt will result in his condemnation and execution, to judge by 4:6–8). This reflects the Roman practice of holding a preliminary hearing, which could result in summary condemnation, but more frequently required a further investigation.

The comprehensive language of desertion in verse 16 reads strangely in the light of Luke's faithful presence (4:11) and of the list of friends from whom Paul will send greetings in verse 21. Perhaps he is speaking not of general support and companionship but of the specific need for legal defence, but we do not know from whom he might have expected such assistance. At any rate, the first part of the trial has been, from the human point of view, a deeply depressing experience of being left to face the music alone. In the circumstances, Paul's prayer, not for revenge but that the desertion may not be counted against them, surely breathes the spirit of his Master (Luke 23:34; compare Acts 7:60); see the comment on 4:14 in Study 35.

But Paul is never alone. When human help evaporates, God is still there. With God's help he has survived the first hearing, and the reference to being given strength (v. 17) and to the proclamation of the message to all the Gentiles suggests that Paul has made good use of the opportunity for public testimony to his Christian convictions. Yet he still expects to be executed (4:6–8). In that case, his confidence in God's continuing protection (v. 18) must refer not to legal acquittal but to Paul's spiritual security. His ultimate destiny in God's 'heavenly kingdom' is assured, even though his ministry on earth is now to be cut short. When Paul is executed, it will not be because God has been defeated. Paul's 'rescue from the lion's mouth' is on a higher plane than mere physical survival.

More friends and colleagues

A few members of Paul's regular team of associates have not been mentioned in 4:10–12, and so we hear now of the whereabouts of two more stalwarts, Erastus (Acts 19:22) and Trophimus (Acts 20:4; 21:29). They too, like Tychicus (and perhaps Crescens and Titus?), are deployed elsewhere in the Christian mission enterprise, and so cannot be with Paul in his imprisonment. Then there are those colleagues who are already in Ephesus with Timothy, the redoubtable couple Prisca (Priscilla) and Aquila (Acts 18:2–3, 18, 26), who were among the most influential early Christian teachers, and whose presence must have been a great strength to Timothy. To them, and to the household of Onesiphorus (whom we considered at 1:16–18), Paul sends greetings.

The shorter list of Roman Christians who send greetings to Timothy (v. 21) along with Paul perhaps indicates the degree of Paul's isolation now in his imprisonment: compare the lavish list of Christians in Rome to whom Paul himself had been able to send greetings in earlier days, even before he himself had visited the city (Romans 16:3–16). The New Testament tells us nothing more about any of the four people named in verse 21, though tradition has it that Linus became bishop of Rome in succession to Peter.

Most readers skip over the lists of personal news and greetings which occur in most of Paul's letters, but they are not without value to us. Recurring names allow us to piece together interesting sketches of the ministry of quite a number of otherwise unknown first-century Christian workers, and to realize that the Pauline mission was very far from being a solo effort by Paul himself. He was the spider at the centre of a widespread and carefully organized web. And even where we know nothing more about the people mentioned, the mere fact that they are there fills in the human dimension of the dynamic early Christian fellowship, and shows us Paul the missionary fanatic as also a man capable of wide and lasting friendship—a man who offered, and needed to receive, human support alongside his paramount trust in God.

PRAYER

'The Lord stood by me and gave me strength.' Help us to expect that, and to experience it in all our circumstances, but especially when human support is lacking. Amen.

37 TITUS 1:1–4

'*The* FAITH WE SHARE'

Each of the letters to Timothy, like all Paul's other letters, begins with words of greeting which go well beyond formal identification of the sender and the recipient. All these greetings breathe the atmosphere of Christian faith and prayer. But the greeting to Titus is fuller and more theologically weighted than those to Timothy, and deserves a special study in its own right before we turn to the 'business' part of the letter.

Personal matters

Paul describes himself not merely as an apostle of Jesus Christ, as he usually does, but also (as in Romans and Philippians) as God's 'servant' (v. 1)—the word really means 'slave'. In this letter, as always, he will be speaking with apostolic authority and expecting to be obeyed, but that authority is not his own: he too is merely a slave, under orders to God his Master.

He describes Titus (as he did Timothy in 1 Timothy 1:2) as his 'loyal child in the faith' (v. 4). Both men were close associates of Paul, and it is likely that Titus, like Timothy, first heard the Christian gospel from Paul the missionary. But whereas we know a little about how Paul 'discovered' Timothy, Titus appears on the New Testament scene as a fully fledged apostolic associate, particularly as Paul's special emissary to Corinth, where he had a very demanding role in trying to bring the wayward Corinthian church back to order (see frequent references in 2 Corinthians). His only earlier appearance in the New Testament story is when he accompanied Paul and Barnabas to Jerusalem as something of an 'exhibit' as a Gentile convert (Galatians 2:1–5). By this time, Titus and Paul have been through a lot together, and Paul has judged him the right man to take up another responsible role in Crete, as he had previously in Corinth.

God's purpose and Paul's ministry

'The faith we share' (v. 4) is spelled out in verses 1–3, as Paul develops the theme of his apostolic commission. It is, like many of Paul's sentences, a rich collection of theological language which is easier to 'feel' than to analyse! Perhaps we can best approach it by drawing out a few key words and phrases for comment.

Truth with godliness (v. 1). The gospel is about truth, of course; but that truth is not an intellectual end in itself. It is the basis for the faith of God's chosen people and it produces godliness of life, not just soundness of thinking. One of Paul's recurring problems throughout these letters is with people who claim to be teaching the truth but whose lives belie the claim. That is not the truth of the gospel.

The hope of eternal life (v. 2). What distinguishes Christians from most other people is that their vision is not limited to this world with all its joys and problems. We are 'strangers and pilgrims' here on earth, and our true life is in God and in heaven. We are people of hope in a hopeless world—and 'hope' in the New Testament does not mean wishful thinking, but a solid, well-grounded expectation.

God who never lies (v. 2). The story of the Bible is the story of promise and fulfilment. God's purpose is older than the world, and its fulfilment as sure as God himself. It may seem to take a very long time from a human perspective, but God knows the 'due time', and when it comes, what was hidden is revealed. That is what has happened with the coming of Jesus Christ.

Entrusted with proclamation (v. 3). Paul's apostolic mission is not to come up with a new scheme for the world's salvation, but to be the herald of what God has already planned and put into operation. It is God's work from first to last, but it includes as an essential ingredient the human messengers who will spread the message so that all may hear. That is the awesome responsibility, and the glory, of the ministry of the gospel, to which both Paul and Titus have been called.

A man who begins a letter like that has got to be worth listening to!

PRAYER

Lord, help me to grasp the 'breadth and length and height and depth, and to know the love of Christ that surpasses knowledge'. Amen.

Ephesians 3:18–19

BLAMELESS 'BISHOPS'

Much of this letter covers similar ground to what we have already seen in the letters to Timothy, and already at the outset of Paul's instructions to Titus we are on familiar ground with the selection of leaders for the local church (1 Timothy 3:1–7). Bear in mind that the two words 'bishop' and 'elder', which for us have quite different connotations, are used in the New Testament to describe the same office (compare vv. 5 and 7). These church leaders were not like our 'bishops', individuals with a primary responsibility for a wide area, but were a group of people called to the shared leadership of a local congregation.

Titus' task

We know nothing of how the church was first founded in Crete. By the end of the story in Acts, there is no indication of any Christians being there. Paul's brief visit to a Cretan port as a prisoner on board ship (Acts 27:7–13) allowed no scope for gospel work. Yet Paul speaks in verse 5 as if he has been in Crete with Titus and has then gone on, leaving Titus behind. This can only have been in the period after the end of the Acts story, between Paul's first and second imprisonments in Rome (see Introduction, p. 12).

Titus' role in Crete is similar to that of Timothy in Ephesus, but at a much earlier stage of the church's development. If Paul's visit had been brief, it may have resulted in the founding of churches but not allowed time to set up the structures needed to maintain them. That is what Titus must now look after. In particular, the appointment of local church leaders, which was normally an early part of Paul's concern for his new churches (Acts 14:23), and which had been done in Ephesus long before Timothy took up his post there (Acts 20:17), had not yet happened in Crete. Moreover, while Ephesus was a single city (admittedly a large and important one), Crete is a large island, and the reference to 'every town' in verse 5 means that churches had been founded throughout the island.

Criteria for leadership

The qualities Titus must look for are virtually the same as those we have already looked at in 1 Timothy 3:1–7, though some are differently expressed or more fully explained. The test of the candidate's children is even more searching here (v. 6): not only are they to be well disciplined and respectful, but they must be themselves believers, and must not have a reputation for wild or rebellious behaviour. This is a tough criterion: we all know children from good Christian homes who have chosen a different way despite their parents' prayers and efforts. But Paul does not want Titus to take risks with the health or with the public reputation of the church. Better safe than sorry.

The reason for this extreme caution is that the church leader is not just someone who must get on well with other church members: he is 'God's steward', responsible for God's household, and so his character must reflect the God he represents. Both the negative qualities of verse 7 and the positive qualities of verse 8 will speak to those he meets of the nature of God himself. A person who lives like that cannot but commend the gospel, and be a powerful example of godliness to those he leads.

But good leadership involves word as well as character. So the people chosen must also have a sound understanding of the 'word that is trustworthy' (v. 9), the apostolic teaching both in its theological and its ethical dimensions. Only such a person will be able to instruct other church members with 'sound doctrine' ('healthy', 'wholesome' teaching, as in 2 Timothy 4:3), and will have the confidence and the intellectual ammunition with which to resist the currents of false teaching which, as we shall soon see, were as serious a problem in Crete as Timothy was finding them in Ephesus.

These are searching criteria. I wonder how many of today's candidates for ministry would be selected by this yardstick.

FOR REFLECTION

You may not be a church leader, but nevertheless let the qualities listed, especially in verses 7 and 8, broaden your vision of Christian maturity. Can you see them developing in your own life, and in other members of your church?

39

TITUS 1:10–16

Portrait *of the* Opposition

Already in the letters to Timothy we have become used to quite lurid portraits of the people whose ideas and behaviour Paul sees as a threat to the healthy development of the church in Ephesus. In Crete the matter seems to be little different, and a reading of these verses leaves a very similar impression. As at Ephesus, while the problem begins with wrong ideas and wrong teaching, it is the behaviour of these people which worries Paul as much as their thinking. Moreover, it is not their ideas alone which draw his criticism, but their motives in fostering their perverted brand of the faith.

Wrong ideas

While Paul is clear that they are teaching 'what it is not right to teach' (v. 11), he is not very explicit about what that teaching is. Twice he mentions their Jewish connections ('those of the circumcision', v. 10; 'Jewish myths', v. 14), and in the light of problems which surface in other first-century letters it seems likely that here was a group of people who emphasized the Jewish pedigree of Christianity to the extent of requiring non-Jewish converts to follow Old Testament laws, especially the food laws, which Paul and the Christians in Jerusalem had long ago decided were not binding on Gentiles (Acts 15). This was a recurring and very sensitive issue in Paul's ministry, and comes to the surface most violently in Galatians. But it goes all the way back to the teaching of Jesus himself, who insisted that 'uncleanness' was a matter of the heart, not of food (Mark 7:14–23), and to Peter's vision which taught him not to stigmatize certain food as 'unclean' (Acts 10:9–16). So when Paul declares (v. 15) that to the 'pure' (or 'clean'—the same Greek word) all things are pure, he is probably declaring his position against those who insisted on continuing to brand certain food as 'unclean' (as in Leviticus 11).

Such teaching (and no doubt there were other such issues being promoted) was inevitably divisive, and Paul is concerned about its effect in 'upsetting whole families'. Such talk is dangerous.

Wrong motives

Perhaps the imputation of unworthy motives is too regular a feature of academic and political debate for us to take it too seriously, but Paul does rather pile it on. These people are 'rebellious, idle talkers and deceivers' (v. 10), they 'reject the truth' (v. 14), they are 'corrupt and unbelieving', with 'corrupted minds and consciences' (v. 15), 'detestable and disobedient' (v. 16), and their religious profession is insincere. More specifically, they are promoting their ideas 'for sordid gain' (v. 11). The charge of mercenary teaching is one which Paul himself was always careful to avert by refusing to accept payment from those whom he taught. These people have not been so scrupulous.

Paul must have chuckled when he discovered in the works of the ancient Cretan poet Epimenides (sixth century BC) the line he quotes in verse 12. What a 'testimony' to come from their own revered sage! Paul's simple comment, 'That testimony is true' perhaps reflects his own unhappy experiences when preaching the gospel in Crete.

Wrong behaviour

If a religious profession leaves a person's life unchanged, it is hollow. Remember the comment in 2 Timothy 3:5 about 'holding to the outward form of godliness but denying its power'? So in verse 16 Paul's charge is that these people's lives deny what their words profess. Their religion is merely skin-deep. He does not go into detail, but perhaps the reference to 'commandments of those who reject the truth' (v. 14) points to a 'religion' based merely on dos and don'ts instead of on the new values of the gospel as Paul has summarized them in 1:1–3 and the transformed nature which he expects especially of church leaders (1:7–8). In chapter 2 he will go on to spell out the way Christians ought to live.

PRAYER

May our lives never deny the truth we profess
and the God we claim to know. Amen.

40 TITUS 2:1–10

DUTIES *of* VARIOUS GROUPS

In contrast with the inappropriate behaviour promoted by his opponents, Titus is to put before the members of the church clear guidelines for Christian living (note again the term 'sound doctrine' or 'wholesome teaching' in verse 1: real Christian teaching results in good living).

He focuses on four groups—older men, older women, younger men, and slaves. But since what he says about older women in fact focuses largely on the behaviour they are to promote among the younger women, the coverage is quite comprehensive (except for children).

Older men and older women

The qualities listed for the older men (v. 2) contain no surprises. They are the sort of words which command immediate assent, and Paul does not feel it necessary to go into detail. One word worth noting is, yet again, the word 'sound', literally 'healthy', which Paul has used repeatedly to characterize good teaching, and which now describes the faith, love and endurance of Christian men, as they are based on that 'sound' teaching.

It is interested that it is the older women specifically (v. 3) who are warned against being 'slanderers' (gossiping?) and, literally, 'enslaved to much wine'. Not that Paul approved of anyone over-indulging in drink (though he approved and even recommended a moderate use, 1 Timothy 5:23), but he seems to have felt that the sight of drunken older women was particularly degrading and dishonouring to their Christian profession. In this, as in all that they do as well as what they say, they are to set an example for younger women to follow.

Younger women and younger men

Both groups are to be 'self-controlled', a general term for appropriate behaviour as opposed to a wild and undisciplined lifestyle. For the women there are further duties especially relating to their families (vv. 4–5). (Note that in the social situation of that time it is taken for granted that younger women will be married; singles do not come into Paul's purview.) They must, as we would expect, love their husbands and children, and be faithful ('chaste'). But Paul also insists on a 'traditional' role relationship, in that the wife's place is in the home, under her husband's authority. 'Good managers of the household' (v. 5) is more literally 'good house-workers', and seems to envisage a domestic rather than public role for the wife, while the ideal of 'submission' reflects Paul's regular insistence on a wife's acceptance that the husband is head of the family. How, if at all, this model of marriage can be made to work in the very different society we know today remains one of the most sensitive questions in Christian ethics!

No more is said directly about the duties of younger men, but Titus (presumably himself a 'younger man') is to provide a role model (vv. 7–8), in ways quite similar to what Paul has already said about older men. Note that at the heart of Paul's concern is the reputation of the church among people outside. Christian behaviour must give no scope for legitimate criticism.

Slaves

Paul has talked about the duties of slaves in 1 Timothy 6:1–2, and in the comments on that passage we have thought about the way New Testament teaching views the institution of slavery, and of the way it was eventually to be undermined by Christian values. But that is still far in the future as Paul writes to Titus, and his concern is not the reform of the system, but the way Christian slaves should behave within it. They are, in a word, to be good slaves who in every way 'give satisfaction' (v. 9), not awkward and unreliable as slaves could so often be. Paul's concern is again with the reputation of the Christian community and therefore of the gospel. Good behaviour, for slaves as for other church members, is a means of 'adorning' the gospel. The principle is that of Matthew 5:16, 'that they may see your good works and give glory to your Father in heaven'.

FOR REFLECTION

As times change and the structures and expectations of society develop in new ways, some of Paul's more specific instructions will not 'fit' directly with our situations. But it is possible to work out the principles which led him to these instructions.
Think about what motives lie behind his specific directions, and how we may give practical 'cash value' to those same principles in our different way of life.

41 TITUS 2:11–15

God's Special People

In these verses Paul fills in the theological background to the instructions he has just been giving. The reason why Christians must behave in a special way is that they are special people. They are the end-product of God's long-term plan of salvation.

Salvation has come

The Christian Church is not a human initiative. It has its origin in 'the grace of God' (v. 11), that free, sovereign decision of God to extend his love and mercy to undeserving humanity. The theme was not a new one at the time of Paul, of course. The story of the Old Testament is the story of God's grace extended again and again, and of the chequered history of his people's response, sometimes in love and loyalty but more often in rebellion against their Creator. But when Paul speaks of the grace of God as 'having appeared', he is thinking of that decisive new phase in God's plan for the world which began with the coming of Jesus to 'bring life and immortality to light', as he said in 2 Timothy 1:10. And that grace of God is (literally) 'saving for all people'. It is the ultimate solution to all the problems of humanity.

Living in hope

But salvation is a process, not just a single once-for-all transaction. While it takes effect powerfully for the people of God in the present age, its ultimate fulfilment still lies in the future, in the 'manifestation of Jesus Christ' (v. 13). There is an element of provisionality in all Christian experience, a strong sense of 'now and not yet'. We live between the ages, looking back to the coming of salvation in the first coming of Christ, but living still in the 'blessed hope' of a second coming in glory.

In expressing this blessed hope, Paul, almost incidentally, lets slip one of the most explicit statements in the New Testament that Jesus, true (Jewish) man that he was, was also much more than that: 'our great God and Saviour'. The language is so unexpected and unguarded in the light of the general reluctance of the New Testament actually to call Jesus 'God' that many have suggested that the words should be read as 'the great God and our Saviour Jesus Christ', but this unnatural rendering of the Greek is unconvincing and unnecessary. While direct statements that Jesus is God are few (though they are there), there is no doubt that that is how the New Testament writers, and particularly Paul, understood the matter, however long it may have taken their language to catch up with their theology!

A people for God

The purpose of Jesus' coming and self-sacrifice was 'to purify for himself a people of his own' (v. 14), set free from evil and 'zealous for good deeds'. The theme of God's special people runs through the Old Testament, as does the disappointment of God when Israel so often failed to live up to that calling. Now Jesus has come to make that plan a reality, and Paul and Titus and the Cretan Christians (and you and I) are part of that new reality. No wonder Paul is so keen to make sure that the members of the Cretan churches do not again let God down.

Living in the present age

So that is why Titus must spare no effort to bring the church members into line. He cannot afford to be ignored, but must boldly exercise his authority as an authorized leader and representative of the apostle (v. 15). He must root out the 'impiety and worldly passions' (v. 12) which characterize life outside, and insist on the 'self-controlled, upright and godly' behaviour which is alone appropriate to the special people of God. The ultimate fulfilment of God's purpose of salvation for them may still be in the future, but already here 'in this present age' their distinctive character must be seen. God expects no less.

PRAYER

Thank you, Lord, for the story of our salvation and for the 'blessed hope' in which we now live. Help us so to grasp what it all means that we may get our lives into perspective, and live as your special people. Amen.

42 TITUS 3:1–7

NEW LIFE *in* CHRIST

The new life—and the old

In verses 1–2 Paul spells out more fully the way Christians are expected to behave, especially in their relations with other people in the community. These verses are about good citizenship. Even though they are the special people of God, they are not to cut themselves off from the rest of society, but to play their part in its life and to make their mark by constructive involvement rather than by separation. They will be conspicuous as law-abiding and responsible citizens. 'Ready for every good work' suggests not merely keeping out of trouble, but actively looking for ways to help. And they will get on well with other people, showing respect and consideration and avoiding conflict and unpleasantness.

All this is in direct contrast with the old life they have left behind when they decided to follow Christ. The sort of character described in verse 3 succeeds only in causing trouble and in making life miserable for others (and indeed often enough for oneself). It is the root of social division and conflict. Paul looks back on the old life with sorrow—and with gratitude to God for saving him from it.

Transformation

The 'goodness and loving kindness' of God (v. 4) is the same as the 'grace' Paul talked about in 2:11, and again the verb 'appeared' indicates that he is thinking of the decisive new phase in God's dealings with humanity which Jesus has brought. It is a divine rescue mission, lifting us out of the hopeless self-centredness of the old life into a new relationship with God, and setting our sights not on this world but on the 'hope of eternal life' (v. 7) which puts everything else into perspective.

Paul, like several other writers in the New Testament, describes this transformation as a new birth, and sets out here the basis, the means and the result of this new birth.

The basis of the new birth

'Not because of any works of righteousness that we had done' (v. 5). This theme is developed at length in the early chapters of Romans: we cannot earn our salvation. Attempts to keep the law only show up the extent of our own failure. Our only hope is not in ourselves but in God. And that is where grace comes in, the free mercy of God which offers new life to those who do not deserve it. 'Justified by his grace' (v. 7) sums up the message of Romans 1—8 in a nutshell.

The means of new birth

It is, of course, through the work of Christ that we find forgiveness of sins and peace with God, as Paul spells out more fully elsewhere. Here, however, he focuses more directly on how we experience this new beginning. 'The washing of rebirth and renewal by the Holy Spirit' (v. 5) is the language of baptism, and draws out the two aspects of baptism which were distinguished originally by John the Baptist, baptism in water and baptism by the Holy Spirit. John himself could offer only the one, the outward symbol of a new beginning by means of water, washing off the old to make way for the new. But he spoke of someone who would come after him and bring the real thing, baptism by the Holy Spirit. This is no longer a merely outward act, but inward, spiritual renewal. And this Spirit has been 'poured out on us richly through Jesus Christ our Saviour' (v. 6). Christian baptism is the symbol of much more than turning over a new leaf—it marks the beginning of a new life.

The result of the new birth

New birth leads to new life, and this new life is not for this world only. It is 'eternal life'. So those who have come to new birth through Jesus Christ have entered a new family, and they have new prospects which were previously out of their reach. They are heirs not of an earthly fortune, but of something far more valuable, the hope of eternal life.

Of course there is far more which a full account of Christian salvation must include, but in these few verses we have an extraordinarily rich summary of what it means to say that God has saved us.

FOR REFLECTION

'Thanks be to God for his indescribable gift' (2 Corinthians 9:15).
Think about what God has done for us in Christ.
If you were asked to summarize the gospel in a few words,
would it look like Titus 3:4–7?

43 TITUS 3:8–15

FINAL INSTRUCTIONS

Pastoral matters

Verses 8 and 9 add little that is new, but reinforce the message already clearly given. Those who profess Christian faith must be instructed in right behaviour, not only because it is good in itself but also because it is in everyone's interest. The sort of lifestyle Paul has been commending throughout this letter is what makes human society work, and leaves everyone better off. Such wholesome living is worth insisting on.

By contrast, the sort of speculative teaching which has become popular among some people in Crete does no good to anyone and promotes disagreement and conflict. We have heard about an unhealthy interest in 'genealogies' also in Ephesus (1 Timothy 1:4); they are probably part of the Gnostic-type cosmological speculations which were at the heart of much first-century popular philosophy and spirituality. (See my comments on 1 Timothy 6:20, Study 22, where I suggested that a modern equivalent might be some aspects of New Age thinking.) Fascinating as such ideas may be, they are likely to do more harm than good, and are better left alone.

But some people will not be taught, and Paul does not want Titus to waste his energy 'flogging a dead horse'. His advice in verses 10–11 reminds us of Jesus' enigmatic warning against casting pearls before swine (Matthew 7:6). There comes a time when it is no longer worth trying to help some people. If they do not want to know, so be it. This is hard advice to follow, and lays upon us the uncomfortable necessity of deciding when the point of no return has been reached. But perhaps Paul's proposal of a first and second warning before giving up may be a practical help in this.

Personal plans and directions

At the time of writing, Paul is still a free man, able to decide his own movements. This letter must therefore be earlier than 2 Timothy. We meet here a number of members of Paul's circle. Artemas and Zenas (vv. 12–13) are otherwise unknown. Tychicus we have met in 2 Timothy 4:12, still travelling loyally as Paul's emissary in his last imprisonment. Apollos may well be the same learned convert whom we meet in Acts 18:24—19:1, and whose eloquent teaching in Corinth led some of the Corinthians to prefer his ministry to that of Paul (1 Corinthians 1:12; 3:4–6). If so, it is encouraging to find that, despite the opposition which some had attempted to stir up, he is now clearly identified with Paul as a colleague rather than as a rival. Indeed, the request to Titus to send Zenas and Apollos on their way, and to provide for their needs, suggests that it was they who were bringing this letter to Titus. If so, Apollos is now firmly part of the apostolic circle and a trusted emissary.

Verse 14 perhaps illuminates the background to Paul's recurring insistence on the need for people to 'do good works' rather than indulge in useless argument. There are 'urgent needs' to be met, and the continuing development of the Christian mission depends on the members of the churches pulling their weight so as to be able to supply those needs, presumably for hospitality and the cost of travel. Paul, for all his theological and rhetorical flights, was nothing if not a realist! The work must go on, and it cannot go on without the willing contribution of well-motivated church members.

So Paul signs off with his usual greetings, not only to Titus but to 'all who love us in the faith' (v. 15). The Christian Church, not only locally but also across the seas, is a family of faith, in which there is a love shared between its members which is on a different level from normal human regard.

PRAYER

Thank you, Lord, for the privilege of belonging to your Church.
Help us each one to play our part, so that the Church may be the better for our being in it, and the work of the gospel go forward.
Amen.

44 HEBREWS

An ODD SORT *of* LETTER?

The first thing that strikes the reader who comes to Hebrews after reading the letters of Paul is that it doesn't begin like a letter. There is no identification of the writer and the recipient(s), no personal greetings or thanksgiving or prayer, indeed nothing personal at all. (The only other letter in the New Testament which similarly dispenses with the traditional opening formulae is 1 John.) The first time the author addresses his readers directly is in 2:1–4, and even then he diplomatically uses 'we' rather than 'you'. What we find instead is a magnificent opening sentence, one of the richest theological statements in the whole New Testament, which reads more like the beginning of a particularly fine rhetorical or philosophical treatise, and from that moment on the author is launched into a sustained and quite sophisticated theological argument, very unlike the collections of local issues which fill many of the letters of Paul.

At the end, however, there are both personal messages (13:18–19, 22–23) and a very brief concluding greeting. So what began like a sermon ends like a letter. And frequently throughout its thirteen chapters the author turns from more abstract argument to a direct appeal to his readers to beware of spiritual danger and rather to press on in faith (especially 2:1–4; 3:12–13; 4:1, 11; 5:11—6:12; 10:19–39; 12:1–13, 25–29).

So, despite its impressive opening, this is no abstract theological treatise, but a pastoral document, written by a church leader who knows intimately and is deeply concerned about his readers' situation. Indeed the theological argument, detailed and erudite as it is, is not there merely as a matter of intellectual interest. It is there to provide the basis for the pastoral appeals which are the main purpose of the letter. The problem which threatened this particular church was at root a problem of theological understanding, and so as a good pastor the author tackles it at the theological level. Only so can he help his readers to a proper understanding of their situation, and of the dangers which confront them.

A sermon (or sermons) written up?

So some have suggested that what we have here is a sermon, written up and sent off with a few greetings added at the end to make it serve as a letter. Certainly its style often seems more sermon than letter, both in its theological exposition and in its impassioned pastoral appeals. And indeed the author himself describes it as a brief (!) 'word of exhortation' (13:22—a phrase used to describe a synagogue sermon in Acts 13:15). In particular, much of the argument is created by 'preaching on' Psalm 110.

Certainly much of the material of the letter may have had its origin in the author's preaching, but it could hardly have been preached in anything like its present form in any other situation, since, like any good sermon, it is very specifically directed to the unique situation in which the readers found themselves. If it is a sermon, it is a sermon written specifically for them, not one drawn out from stock!

Others have noticed that certain Old Testament passages provide the focus of the argument for sometimes quite lengthy passages. So are we looking not at one sermon but at a collection of several expositions of key texts? The following might be suggested:

2:5–18 as a sermon on Psalm 8:4–6
3:7—4:13 as a sermon on Psalm 95:7–11
5:5—7:28 as a sermon on Psalm 110:4
8:1—10:18 as a sermon on Jeremiah 31:31–34
10:32—12:3 as a sermon on Habakkuk 2:3–4
12:4–13 as a sermon on Proverbs 3:11–12
12:18–29 as a sermon on the Sinai story in Exodus

In each case the author works with and returns to the key text, in a way quite like some modern expository preaching, with Psalm 110 as his primary text to which he frequently returns.

So perhaps we may best describe Hebrews as a letter indeed, but a letter with a difference, written by an experienced preacher and expositor, and drawing on his regular preaching ministry to find the arguments which this particular group of Christians needed to hear.

FOR REFLECTION

People sometimes talk as if 'academic' and 'pastoral' concerns were separate and even in conflict with one another. Is this an appropriate division? Which side of it do you think Hebrews belongs?

45 HEBREWS

Who Wrote Hebrews?

In the Introduction to this volume, we noticed that Hebrews is an anonymous document, and that while some church tradition credited it to Paul, there is nothing in the letter to say so, and its style is quite unlike the letters of Paul.

Early Christian views of Hebrews

So people soon began guessing who the author of this impressive document might be: names such as Luke, Barnabas and Clement were suggested. But surely the most appropriate verdict among the early Church Fathers was that of Origen, writing in the third century, who commented that the thoughts might be those of Paul, but the style and composition derived from someone else, and went on, 'But who actually wrote the epistle, God knows'!

What mattered most for these early church leaders was not so much the identity of the author as the quality of the work, which so strongly undergirded the apostolic teaching. Despite its very distinctive style and atmosphere, they did not doubt that Hebrews was an authentic representative of orthodox Christian theology.

Modern thoughts about Hebrews

Martin Luther in the sixteenth century was the first person to suggest what has since become the favourite theory, that it was Apollos who wrote Hebrews. We shall return to this in a moment.

Plenty of other suggestions have been made, one of the most interesting being that of Adolf von Harnack that the author was Priscilla, who, with her husband Aquila, was responsible for instructing Apollos in the faith (Acts 18:24–26). Priscilla was certainly a significant partner in the Christian mission in the first century, and the idea of a female author of a New Testament book is attractive, but it remains a guess, and unfortunately the author uses a masculine participle of himself in 11:32.

But the letter remains anonymous, and there seems no reason to suppose that the author must be one of the very limited group of first-century Christian leaders whose names we know. It is clearly the work of a theologian of some stature, and a person with original and fascinating ideas. Modern scholars sometimes speak of its author along with Paul and John as the three great theologians of the New Testament. But we do not know who he or she was; we must content ourselves with talking simply about 'the author'.

Why Apollos was a good guess

From the contents of the letter we may deduce quite a lot about what sort of person wrote it. He (and from now on I shall resist the temptation always to say 'he or she'!) was Jewish to his fingertips, deeply learned in the Old Testament, a scholar with a subtle philosophical mind and a fine grasp of Greek idiom and style. Some of the language he uses is similar to that of Philo, the first-century Jewish philosopher from Alexandria, and the author must have been well acquainted with Alexandrian thought (as opposed to the more conservative Judaism of Palestine). But he is a clear-sightedly *Christian* Jew, and experienced in controversy with non-Christian Jews. And he is a caring and conscientious Christian pastor.

Apollos fits this portrait remarkably well: a learned Jew of Alexandria, 'eloquent', 'well-versed in the scriptures', an enthusiastic propagandist for 'the Way of the Lord' even before he was taken and given a grounding in more orthodox theology by Priscilla and Aquila (Acts 18:24–26). Thereafter, he travelled around the Mediterranean as a preacher and church leader, 'powerfully refuting the Jews in public, showing by the scriptures that the Messiah is Jesus' (Acts 18:27–28). His influence at Corinth was great, bidding fair to eclipse even that of Paul (1 Corinthians 1:12; 3:4–9, 22; 4:6); hence perhaps Paul's rather self-conscious explanation to the Corinthians of why he had deliberately avoided eloquence and philosophical argument (1 Corinthians 1:17—2:5).

Such a man could well have written Hebrews. But of course we don't know whether he did!

PRAYER

We thank you, Lord, for so many faithful and gifted men and women through whom we have received your truth. May we in our turn use all our gifts and efforts to pass on the faith in a way that speaks to our generation as they did to theirs. Amen.

46 HEBREWS

WHO WERE 'THE HEBREWS'?

The traditional title of the letter, 'To the Hebrews', even though not part of the letter itself, is surely right as far as it goes. It is written to Jewish Christians. But just who they were, or where, is not stated. This is not a sort of encyclical to all Jewish Christians, but rather an urgent letter to a particular group facing a crisis situation. They may have been quite a small group, a sort of 'house church', rather than representing all the Christians in their town.

The greeting from 'those from Italy' (13:24) most likely suggests that the recipients were in Italy (and therefore receiving greetings from their expatriate friends), and, if so, the most likely location would be Rome. We know from Paul's letter to the Romans that there was a substantial Jewish element in the Roman church, and it may have been a group of those, meeting together as what would now be called a 'Messianic congregation', to whom the letter was sent.

A danger of apostasy

It is clear from the letter that this group are under severe pressure and are seriously considering abandoning their Christian profession. There has been active persecution (10:32–34; 12:3–4), and probably also the less direct but ultimately more powerful pressure of ideological isolation from their fellow Jews. Most Jews who decided to follow Jesus in the first century found themselves accused of treachery and of going off after 'the deceiver', and yet at the same time could be regarded with suspicion by Gentile Christians who, following Paul's teaching, rejoiced in their 'freedom from the law'. To be a Jewish Christian in the first century was likely to be an uncomfortable position, as indeed it has been found by many right up to the present day.

External pressure might, of course, merely serve to strengthen their resolve to follow Christ. But the tone of the letter sometimes suggests that they themselves may have been wondering whether they had been right in deciding to follow Jesus.

It is hard for those who have never belonged to another religious community to understand the pull which a person's cultural and religious 'roots' may continue to exert even after a conversion experience. They could not cease to be Jewish. Indeed they ought not to, since the Christian faith is not a totally new invention, but is the fulfilment of God's dealings with Israel. There is a vital element of continuity which only a Jewish Christian can fully appreciate. But when you see your fellow Jews continuing contentedly in their religion without recourse to the new teaching of Jesus, and find that they regard you as having abandoned your Jewish identity, it may need a strong conviction of the rightness of the Christian claim to keep you on course. It is that conviction which apparently these 'Hebrews' lacked, and it is the main purpose of this letter to supply it, to prove that Jesus is the fulfilment, not the abandonment, of Israel's heritage.

Some have suggested, in the light of the strong focus on sacrificial ritual and on the role of the Old Testament priests, that these 'Hebrews' were former priests who had decided to follow Jesus (compare Acts 6:7); such converts would be particularly obvious targets for persecution. But the sort of pressure which this letter reflects would have been well known among Jewish Christians of all sorts, especially perhaps those who lived in a place like Rome where the majority of Christians were Gentiles, but where a strong continuing Jewish community could make life uncomfortable for Jews who now followed Jesus.

When?

It is a remarkable fact that a letter whose argument depends on the need to leave behind the old phase of religion, and which emphasizes that the Old Testament priesthood and its sanctuary have now been superseded and that the old covenant is 'obsolete' (8:13), none the less manages to avoid any reference to the destruction of the Jerusalem temple which took place in AD70. It would have been such an obvious 'QED' argument that it is easier to believe that it had not yet happened at the time of writing than that the author studiously avoided mentioning such a obviously relevant point. In that case, the letter was probably written some time in the sixties of the first century.

FOR REFLECTION

Think about the difference between being a Gentile Christian and a Jewish Christian today. Do you know any Jewish Christians? What are the special aspects of the Christian faith and of Christian experience for them?

47 HEBREWS

What Is Hebrews All About?

In the last study, we thought about what seems to have been the special situation which the first readers of this letter faced, and the danger they were in. There was a serious possibility that they might 'drift away' (2:1) from their Christian faith. Sometimes the author puts it more strongly: they are in danger of 'falling away' by 'crucifying again the Son of God and holding him up to contempt' (6:6), of 'spurning the Son of God, profaning the blood of the covenant, and outraging the Spirit of grace' (10:29) and 'refusing the one who is speaking' (that is, God) (12:25). The letter is a solemn warning that 'it is a fearful thing to fall into the hands of the living God' (10:31) because 'our God is a consuming fire' (12:29).

That sounds pretty forbidding, and Hebrews is nothing if not a serious document. But most of the letter is taken up not with these lurid warnings, but with a careful explanation of just why it is right to follow Jesus, of the privilege of being his people.

The main theme

There was a popular song many years ago which had the refrain 'Anything you can do, I can do better.' For 'you' put the religion of the Old Testament, and for 'I' put Christ, and you have an excellent summary of what Hebrews is all about. And it is that word 'better' which keeps on surfacing in this letter so that it becomes a sort of refrain: 'better' than the angels (1:4); 'a better hope' (7:19); 'a better covenant' (7:22; 8:6); 'better promises' (8:6); 'better sacrifices' (9:23); a 'better and more lasting' possession (10:34); 'a better country' (11:16); 'a better resurrection' (11:35); the blood of Jesus which 'speaks better than the blood of Abel' (12:24). It is all summed up when the author concludes his great roll-call of the heroes of faith in the Old Testament by saying that even they did not receive what God had promised, 'since God had provided something better so that they would not, apart from us, be made perfect' (11:40).

That is what it means to be a Christian—to be living in the days of fulfilment, for which even the very best of Old Testament faith was merely a foreshadowing. And they were thinking of giving that up!

The development of the argument

To establish this point, the author works his way through some of the most important elements of Old Testament religion, the points of particular pride for a Jew, and shows how in each case something 'better' has been given to us in the coming of Jesus, God's Son through whom he is speaking his last word to humanity. Some sections are more complex than others, and include subsidiary arguments (notably the famous discussion of Melchizedek in chapter 7), but a rough outline is as follows:

1:1–3	Better than the prophets
1:4—2:18	Better than the angels
3:1—4:13	Better than Moses and Joshua
4:14—7:28	Better than the Old Testament priesthood
8:1–13	Better than the old covenant
9:1—10:18	Better than the sacrificial system

From 10:19 on he turns from argument to exhortation, calling on his readers to enter into and enjoy this 'new and living way', but still the theme of 'betterness' recurs, as he shows how all the great heroes of faith in the Old Testament represent only a preliminary stage in God's purpose (ch. 11), and contrasts the glory of the new 'Mount Zion' of Christian salvation with the terrors of the 'Mount Sinai' of the old covenant (12:18–24). Only in chapter 13 does he allow himself to be diverted from this overriding theme to deal with a few more local matters of instruction.

If you look back at the list of 'expositions' of key Old Testament texts which I gave in Study 44, you will see how they tie in with these main divisions of the argument, each text serving to illustrate a new aspect of 'betterness'. I will try to draw attention to these links as we work through the text, but I hope this overview of what the letter is all about may help to put it all in perspective.

PRAYER

Thank you, Lord, for the simple clarity of the vision of this author. Help us to get things in perspective as he did, and so not to fail to see the wood of your wonderful plan of salvation for the trees of theological discussion. Amen.

MAKING SENSE *of* HEBREWS

An alien world?

Some people find Hebrews hard going. It speaks of a world very different from ours, a world of animal sacrifices and complex ritual laws, of an ancient tabernacle and its furniture. The stories and teaching of the Old Testament which it takes for granted are not very familiar to most modern Christians, and it all seems very remote even from modern church life, let alone the matters which fill our newspapers.

It is no good pretending that the distance is not there. This is an ancient document, and belongs to a culture long since vanished. Like all ancient literature, it makes demands on modern readers, and calls on us to familiarize ourselves with that lost world if we are to get inside the skin of the author and his first readers. But help is at hand, mainly in the pages of the Old Testament itself. These were the sacred books on which the author and his readers had been brought up, which were second nature to them. So he could refer to them with a confident hope that his readers would know what he was alluding to not only when he quoted texts verbatim but also in the whole mental furniture which underlies his argument.

So I suppose I ought to advise you, unless you are already thoroughly at home in the Old Testament, in its byways as well as its main avenues, to postpone your study of Hebrews until you have undertaken at least a refresher course on the Old Testament! But of course that is not realistic, and in any case that is partly what a commentary like this is for. So I shall try to fill in the background wherever it is needed (with apologies to those who know it all already), and to draw attention to allusions which might escape a modern reader.

Surprising arguments

But the distance of Hebrews from us lies not only in the material with which the author and his readers are familiar, but also in the way he uses it. He shares the conventions of ancient Jewish reading of the scriptures, which was often more creative and subtle than the 'scientific exegesis' which is fashionable today. So he seems to make texts mean things which would have surprised their original authors, and to delight in drawing out imaginative connections between texts and themes on what seem the flimsiest of pretexts.

We shall see plenty of examples of this as we work through the letter. But it is important not to get this out of proportion. Most of the time his use of Old Testament texts would cause no surprise in a modern pulpit, especially his handling of those key texts which form the basis of his extended 'expositions'. He has understood them in their original context and drawn out appropriate themes from them. What is not to be found in the original text, of course, is the new Christian setting to which they must now be applied, and it is in making this application that some of his more creative and even daring new insights can be found. But that is to say no more than that he is reading the Old Testament *as a Christian*, that he is looking back to the foreshadowing in the light of its fulfilment. And that surely is a perspective with which every Christian must be content.

Keeping your bearings

Probably there will be places in this letter when you find the argument unexciting, and feel that he is 'going on a bit'. But let us do the author the courtesy of trying to see things as he saw them, and as he clearly felt his readers needed to see them, even if in the end we conclude that that is not the way we would have wanted to develop the argument or to tackle the pastoral emergency.

And I would be surprised if you do not find in the end that this letter, for all its more obscure patches, sets out a consistent and really rather heart-warming account of what God has done for us in sending his Son, of the new world that has opened up through his sacrifice on the cross, and of the privilege of being the people of the new covenant. Indeed I defy any true Christian to get to the end without a sense of excitement. The journey from here to there may be long, and may have some awkward turnings, but when we get to the end and look back, I hope we shall see it all in true perspective, and agree that it has been supremely worthwhile.

PRAYER

Lord, help me to understand and appreciate what matters, to be content to leave what remains obscure, and to know the difference! Amen.

God's Last Word

There are a few passages in the New Testament which stand out as the supreme statements on the key question of Christian theology—who is Jesus? Think of Paul's poetic summaries in Philippians 2:6–11 and Colossians 1:15–20, or of the magnificent opening verses of John's Gospel. This opening sentence of Hebrews (verses 1–4 are all one sentence in Greek) is right up there with them in the front rank. Indeed, what it says in its special 'Hebrews' way is very similar especially to Colossians 1:15–20 and John 1:1–18.

The prophets and the Son

Israel's religion was based on revelation. Their God was a God who 'spoke', and the prophets through whom that message came were their chief glory. Long ago, in the time of their deliverance from Egypt, they heard God speaking through Moses, and time and again in many different circumstances God raised up these fearless and formidable characters to declare his warnings and his promises with a resounding 'Thus says the Lord'.

But now all that is in the past, and something unimaginably wonderful has come to take its place. 'In these last days' (v. 2) God has sent not a spokesman, but 'a Son'. Remember Jesus' parable of the owner of the vineyard, whose servants were rejected by his tenants, and who in the end, as a last resort, sent his only son (Mark 12:1–6)? Even God cannot go further than this. For as this amazing sentence will go on to unfold, in sending his Son he has in effect sent himself. Or, as John 1:14 puts it, 'The Word became flesh, and lived among us'.

'The Son' is this writer's favourite title for Jesus. In the rest of chapter 1 he will spell out the unique glory of the Son, above even the angels, ranked alone with God himself.

The Son and the creation

To show his readers just how important a person the Son is, the author goes on to talk both about his relation to the created world and about his relation to God himself. Three clauses (vv. 2–3a) spell out how the Son relates to creation.

'Through whom he created the worlds.' Or as John 1:3 puts it, 'All things came into being through him'. In Proverbs 8:22–31 God's Wisdom is portrayed as a person, his companion even before the world was created, and his associate in creation, a 'master-worker' rejoicing in the newly made universe. From this hint, Jewish thought developed the motif of Wisdom personified, the creative power in God's universe. And the New Testament writers delighted to trace in Jesus the incarnation of this Wisdom, the agent in creation.

'Whom he appointed heir of all things.' It is God's world, and because Jesus is his Son it all belongs to him as well. 'All things have been created through him *and for him*' (Colossians 1:16).

'He sustains all things by his powerful word.' Not just the initial creation, but the continuing order and survival of the universe depend on the Son. The Old Testament knows nothing of 'deism', the belief that God created the world and then left it to run itself like a well-wound clock. Rather God is at work day by day in his world; creation is a continuing process. And now we see that this role too is focused in the Son.

The Son and the Father

You might think no bolder claim could be made, but you would be wrong. This Son not only does the creative work of God, but himself reveals God's very nature. The language of the beginning of verse 3 again echoes the way Jews spoke of Wisdom (see, in the Apocrypha, Wisdom 7:25–26). 'Reflection' is more literally 'outshining', God's essential glory radiating out in his Son for all to see; 'exact imprint' translates a word for the impression made by a seal on wax, exactly reproducing the design on the seal. So in the Son we can see just what God is like; in him God is made visible. 'Whoever has seen me has seen the Father' (John 14:9). We have seen 'the light of the knowledge of the glory of God in the face of Jesus Christ' (2 Corinthians 4:6). Belief in the divinity of Jesus cannot be much clearer than that.

FOR REFLECTION

Read Colossians 1:15–20 and compare it with these verses. What do you think our author wanted his readers to conclude from his opening sentence? How far have we grasped its significance even now?

50 HEBREWS 1:3b–5

ABOVE *the* ANGELS

You might be forgiven for feeling a bit breathless at the end of the last passage, but the author is only just getting into his stride. The same Greek sentence which began the letter continues to the end of verse 4, and then, having introduced the subject of angels, he will spend the rest of this chapter exploring just how much greater this incomparable Son is even than the angels.

Why angels?

Some people are surprised to find the author spending so much time on angels. Even if they feature in some popular fiction and films, not many people today take them seriously, or expect them to be part of everyday experience. But for a first-century Jew it was different. God had in the past often communicated with his people through angels, particularly through one special 'Angel of the Lord' who appears from time to time in the Old Testament stories as God's messenger, and sometimes is spoken of as if he were God himself (see, for example, Genesis 16:7–13; Judges 13:2–22). The law was believed to have been brought to Moses by angels (2:2; compare Galatians 3:19). While angels were not an everyday experience, it did not surprise people if God still chose this way to communicate with his people (see Joseph's dreams in Matthew 1—2, or Acts 12:6–11).

So in a letter which aims to show that in Jesus we have something 'better' than all that the old religion could offer, angels have a natural place.

At the right hand of God

A passing reference to the redeeming work of the Son, making 'purification for sins' (v. 3), will be more fully developed in the next chapter, and much more so in chapters 9—10. Here the reference to the cross serves to introduce its sequel, the resurrection and ascension of Jesus to take his seat at God's right hand. This is a position of authority that no one else can share, certainly not angels, however high their place may be in the created order.

Here already, at the very beginning of the letter, we are hearing the language of Psalm 110, which will play so central a role in Hebrews' account of the special significance of Jesus. The psalm begins with God saying to 'my lord', 'Sit at my right hand, until I make your enemies your footstool'. That 'lord' to whom God speaks is clearly the king, and in Jewish understanding of the psalm especially the Messiah, the ultimate God-given ruler of God's people who would supersede all ordinary kings.

Jesus himself interpreted this psalm as referring to his own future glory (Mark 14:62, and compare Mark 12:35–37), and the New Testament writers love to refer to it in the same way, but none so much as the author of Hebrews. He will quote its first verse again in 1:13, and it will be echoed in 8:1; 10:12–13; 12:2, while verse 4 of the psalm will form the basis of his argument about Melchizedek in 5:5—7:28. Here it serves to prove the unique status of the Son, at God's right hand and thus set in authority even over the angels.

Father and Son

With verse 5 we begin a series of seven Old Testament quotations, all designed to establish this same point, the superiority of the Son to the angels—a series which we shall consider mainly in the next study, but which for convenience I have split by taking the first two (which make up verse 5) in this study.

The first is from Psalm 2:7, another psalm about the king-Messiah, but one which this time contributes also the title 'Son'. It is followed by words from 2 Samuel 7:14, part of Nathan's great prophecy to David about how God would build him a 'house', not of stones but of his own descendants. It is David's son who is to be also recognized as God's Son. The immediate reference was no doubt to Solomon, but Jewish interpretation had always understood this promise as looking beyond Solomon to that greater 'son of David', the Messiah, who was still to come.

So, to the image of the creative Wisdom of God these quotations add that of God's unique Son, a special relationship to which no angel can aspire, and which reaches its fulfilment as the Son takes his seat beside the Father's throne, in the place of supreme authority in God's universe.

PRAYER

May we, with the angels, rejoice to recognize the Son upon the throne, and give him all honour and obedience. Amen.

51 HEBREWS 1:6–14

The SUPREMACY *of the* SON

The series of Old Testament quotations continues throughout this passage, and is summed up in verse 14 with the conclusion that angels are merely 'spirits in the divine service', and so cannot be compared with the Son whom they serve.

The two quotations in verses 6 and 7 focus on the status of the angels as servants. The remaining three quotations in verses 8–13, however, make no further mention of angels, but are chosen simply to establish the unique status of the Son in his own right. In these quotations the author does not always understand the words of the text as we do, and in at least two cases the use he makes of that text is quite daringly original.

The angels as servants

The quotation in verse 6 comes from a version of Deuteronomy 32:43 which is different from our Hebrew text, but is found in the much older Hebrew version preserved among the Dead Sea Scrolls. A call for the angels to worship the Son seems to establish the author's point clearly enough, until we realize that the 'him' of the Deuteronomy text is not the Son but God himself. Well, of course the angels are to worship *God*, but what has that to do with the *Son*? And the remarkable truth is that the author has quite simply assumed that what is true of God is true of the Son as well. So he is presupposing the point he sets out to prove, because for him, in the light of what he has just said in verses 2–3, it is obvious that what God is, the Son is, and what is due to God is due also to the Son. The logic is not compelling to anyone who does not share his initial belief, but the fact that he can mount such an argument at all is testimony to how deeply the divinity of the Son is rooted in his mind.

The quotation from Psalm 104:4 in verse 7 uses the standard Greek translation (the Septuagint), which depends on construing the Hebrew words differently from the way our versions take them. In the psalm context, this Greek interpretation seems to us unlikely, but it is one which would have been shared by other Jews at that time who read their Old Testament in Greek. The point of the quotation is again the inferior status of angels, as mere 'servants'.

The glory of the Son

We have already thought about the quotation of Psalm 110:1 in verse 13. If the psalm is understood as referring to the Messiah, then its relevance here is obvious enough: it is as the enthroned Messiah that the Son is to be served by the angels.

Verses 8–9 quote Psalm 45:6–7, the psalm for a royal wedding. It addresses the royal bridegroom in terms which for a mere mortal are wildly extravagant, even daring to address him as 'God'. And yet the very next verse goes on to speak of 'God, *your* God'. So who is this royal figure, who is both identified with and distinguished from God in the psalm? For our author the answer is clear enough: this king, like the kings of Psalms 2 and 110, is no mere human ruler, but the king-Messiah. And it is in the Son that this figure finds its full embodiment.

So far so good. If these royal psalms speak of the Messiah, they may appropriately be pressed into service to demonstrate the supreme authority of the Son. But in Psalm 102, whose verses 25–27 are quoted in verses 10–12, there is no king, no Messiah in sight. The 'Lord' to whom this praise is addressed is quite simply God himself, the Creator. So, as in verse 6, the author has assumed what he has set out to prove. He has already declared in verses 2 and 3 that it was through the Son that God created and sustains the universe. So it follows that anything which is said about the Creator in the Old Testament is really about the Son.

'Creative' interpretation?

I have called such use of the Old Testament 'daringly original', and so it may seem to us. But many first-century Christians had already absorbed so fully the idea of Christ's divinity that they, like many Christians today, could use the term 'Lord' without needing to decide whether that Lord was God or Christ. It is not, perhaps, an argument to convince the unpersuaded, but as a demonstration to Jewish Christians that their 'Lord', the Son, rightly occupied the highest place in the universe, it was more than adequate.

FOR REFLECTION

How far does modern Christian devotion match up to the first Christians' instinctive tendency to treat Jesus as the same as God? In our pursuit of historical realism and of 'scientific exegesis', are we in danger of missing something important?

BEWARE *of* 'DRIFTING'!

We have not yet finished with angels: the rest of chapter 2 will look at them in relation to the Son from a new angle. But first the author draws back from developing his theological theme for the first of several severe warnings to his readers which will punctuate the letter. His theological arguments, which may sometimes seem to modern readers rather esoteric, are there not just for academic interest, but in order to talk his readers out of a dangerous situation. So from time to time his pastoral heart gets the better of his intellectual detachment, and he appeals to them directly.

The danger of 'drifting away'

He is writing to those who have already embraced the Christian faith. We considered in Study 46 the sort of pressures that seem to have been bearing on them, and the temptation to give it all up. Even at this early stage in his argument he has given them sufficient grounds for standing firm in their allegiance to the Son, to whom God has given the supreme power in the universe. But the danger he envisages here is not so much that they might be forced into a direct repudiation of their faith in Jesus, but rather that under the pressure of circumstances they might inadvertently lose their grip. 'Drift away' (v. 1) translates a verb which more literally means to flow past, a very passive, casual, undemanding sort of movement. In verse 3 he warns not against denying the faith but against 'neglecting' it, more literally not caring about it. Their danger is apparently, at least in part, that they will lose out by just not bothering.

The point of this appeal is that the Christian message is far too important for that.

Comparison with the old law

When Moses received the law at Sinai, it was a solemn occasion. In 12:18–21 the author will remind his readers of the awesome manifestations of God's holiness which left the people terrified and even Moses himself trembling. That law carried stringent demands, and people ignored them at their peril. The Old Testament is full of examples of people who, whether deliberately or inadvertently, disobeyed

God's laws and paid the penalty. The God of Sinai was not to be trifled with.

But that was only the old law, given through angels, and (as Hebrews will go on to show in various ways) valid only for a temporary period until that which was better should take its place. Now, with the coming of the one who is greater than the angels, there is the offer of a 'great salvation' (v. 3) on a different level altogether. If the old law was to be taken seriously, this is far more so. To let this 'great salvation' slip, and revert to the old, would be not only extremely foolish, but also dangerous—'How can we escape'?

The witnesses to the new covenant

If angels brought the old law, the gospel comes with far greater attestation. Its first exponent was no less than 'the Lord' himself, Jesus, the Son, whom we have just seen to be far above the angels. But perhaps these Hebrew Christians had not been there in Palestine to hear the Lord in person; never mind, they have also the testimony of those who heard him in the flesh, the apostolic witness which was the basis on which they had come to Christian faith. This is no flimsy tissue of speculation, but a firmly attested tradition of what the historical Jesus did and taught, of how God has spoken to us by a Son (1:1–2).

But there is greater testimony even than that—the testimony of God himself, not by words only but by deeds of power. The 'signs and wonders and miracles' (v. 4) may refer to those recorded in the Gospels, and perhaps also those which continued to accompany the apostolic witness as we see recorded in Acts. But they may also be an appeal to the readers' own memories, to supernatural events in their own experience when they first responded to the gospel. The 'gifts of the Holy Spirit' suggest as much: they have found the Spirit at work among them in ways beyond human explanation.

After all that, what folly even to think of going back!

PRAYER

Lord, may we never lose the wonder of our salvation. Deliver us from 'drifting'. Amen.

53 HEBREWS 2:5–9

LOWER *than the* ANGELS

In chapter 1 the author argued for the superiority of Jesus because he was *above* the angels. Now in chapter 2, with a neatly paradoxical twist, he argues that he is superior also because he was, for a time, *below* them. It all depends on Psalm 8, that wonderful hymn to God the Creator.

The message of Psalm 8

The theme of the psalm is the majesty of God the Creator, the sovereign over all the earth. As the psalmist contemplates the immensity of God's creation, he is overwhelmed with a sense of the insignificance of human beings. And yet, he knows, God is concerned for them, and even more than that, he has given them a special responsibility, to look after his world for him. So humanity, for all its littleness, has a place of honour only a little below God himself, and in authority over all the rest of creation.

Finding Jesus in Psalm 8

The psalm does not look like promising ground for an argument about Jesus (or indeed about angels). But there are two features in its wording which open up theological possibilities.

The first is that Psalm 8:4 refers to human beings by the term 'the son of man' (though some of our modern versions which use inclusive language do not show this). The Hebrew phrase does mean just that, a 'human being', or 'humanity' collectively, but it was also the phrase that Jesus chose as a special title for himself, and no Christian reader could now come across the phrase without thinking of Jesus. Here then is the first clue, but Hebrews does not simply take advantage of the word-play, but turns it into a theological argument. The dominion which God promised to human beings does not yet seem to have been established for humanity as a whole (v. 8), but instead 'we see Jesus', in whom this human destiny is now to be fulfilled.

So the title 'the son of man' does in fact point to a real connection—a solidarity of Jesus with humanity—and in the rest of this chapter it is this solidarity which will be explored to explain how Jesus, the divine Son, was able none the less to become the saviour of his human family.

What about the angels?

Our English versions of Psalm 8:5 speak of humanity as being 'a little lower than God', but the Hebrew word for 'God' is plural, and ancient interpreters of the psalm understood it here to be speaking not of God but of other spiritual beings, the angels. That is what the Greek version used by Hebrews says. So humanity's place of honour is measured in relation to the angels, just below their level. But what happens when we see Jesus, who is greater than the angels, taking the place of humanity? Here the author finds a clue in the phrase 'a little lower', and reads the phrase 'a little' as a statement of time (as the Hebrew phrase allows, however unlikely it is to mean that in this context). It thus becomes a reference to the temporary situation into which Jesus entered by becoming a man, leaving his superior status in order to be 'for a little while lower than the angels' (v. 7).

More creative interpretation?

Yes, our author has found meaning in this psalm which is pretty certainly not what the psalmist meant. How could he mean this, living centuries before the coming of Jesus as the 'son of man'? This is not scientific exegesis, but the delight of a subtle interpreter in discovering Jesus in the Old Testament by Christian hindsight.

But the theology which he has drawn from the psalm is centrally important to Christian faith. By being willing to become for a time lower than the angels, the Son of God has identified himself with us humans, and so is now able to do for us what no angel could do, to become our saviour. And that identification has brought him to the lowest point of humiliation, that of 'tasting death for everyone' (v. 9). It is only because Jesus 'stooped to conquer' and became one of us that we can find salvation through his suffering. That is the theme which this chapter will go on to explore.

FOR REFLECTION

O generous love! that he, who smote
In Man for man the foe,
The double agony in Man
For man should undergo.

John Henry Newman (1801–90)

Jesus, Our Elder Brother

The creative interpretation of Psalm 8 has opened up a new avenue for our understanding of the great salvation God has brought to us in his Son, and also of why Jesus is so much better than the angels. In chapter 1 it was his eternal, divine glory which set him apart from them. In this chapter it is his humiliation, his willingness to come down below the level of the angels, to share the lot of humanity, which makes him 'better', because only by this means could he be our saviour. This is the theme that the author is now developing.

'Perfect'

In verse 10 we meet for the first time a word which will be important in this letter, 'perfect'. It comes as a surprise to find the idea that Jesus had to be 'made perfect' (the idea will be expressed more fully in 5:7–10). Does this suggest that there was a time when Jesus was not perfect? Christian theology would find that difficult, and so would our author, who in common with the other New Testament writers has no doubt that Jesus was always 'without sin' (4:15).

The problem is that we tend to think of 'perfection' in moral terms, as the opposite of 'morally flawed'. But that is not at all what our author means. He is talking about God's age-long purpose of salvation, which has now in Christ reached the stage of completion, 'perfection' (9:9; 10:1, 14; 11:40). And in order to fulfil that purpose it was necessary for Christ to be fully equipped ('made perfect') for his role as saviour. Before he became one of us he could not save us, any more than the angels could; by becoming man and dying for us he has become 'perfect' for the job.

Jesus the pioneer

God has many children to 'bring to glory', but on that road to glory they need someone to lead them, to open up a new way which they can follow (see 10:19–20). So Jesus, who has come to take us home, is our 'pioneer' or, as 12:2 will put it, 'the pioneer and perfecter of our faith'. He has gone before us as an example of living the life of faith, but that is not the main point. He has opened a way where there was none before. He has made our salvation possible by what he has done for us. And he has done it by his sufferings, 'tasting death for everyone' (2:9), a theme which our author will explore more fully in chapters 9 and 10.

That is why, at the beginning of verse 11, a distinction is drawn between Jesus and his people. He is the 'sanctifier', and they are the 'sanctified'. However strongly the author may emphasize the solidarity of Jesus with us as our brother—and this is a vital part of his argument—a distinction remains. When it comes to our salvation, he is the subject and we are the objects. He has done for us what we could not do for ourselves.

Brothers and sisters

None the less, it is Jesus' solidarity with us that the author wants to emphasize at this point. It was only because Jesus shared our life and our sufferings that he was able to take our place in his redeeming suffering and death. He came among us not as an alien being (as an angel would have done) but as one of us. That is why the theme of Jesus our brother is so important. It is not a theme which the New Testament often emphasizes, but without it there is no basis for our salvation. Jesus had to be 'like his brothers and sisters in every respect' (v. 17).

Instinctively the author turns to the Old Testament again for backing for this element in his theology. The first text he chooses (v. 12) is Psalm 22:22. This is the great passion psalm, quoted by Jesus on the cross and echoed at several points in the Gospel stories of Jesus' passion. If the suffering psalmist represents the suffering and dying Messiah, then it is significant that, when the psalm turns to praise for God's deliverance, he refers to his fellow worshippers as his 'brothers and sisters' ('brothers' in the original being used, as usual in the Bible, as an inclusive term). The other text, Isaiah 8:17–18 (v. 13), is less obviously appropriate, as it refers to the prophet's children rather than brothers, but perhaps it serves to underline the idea of a family relationship shared between Jesus and his people.

PRAYER

Thank you, Lord Jesus, for becoming one of us. Thank you for the perfect salvation you have achieved. Thank you for being our pioneer, and our brother. Help us to follow where you lead, and to live as fellow members of God's family. Amen.

The PERFECT SAVIOUR

Flesh and blood

The theme of Jesus' solidarity with us continues. He had to be just like us, to share our situation and our experiences, so that he could bring salvation into that human scene. So he shared our 'flesh and blood' (v. 14), he shared the experience of death, the 'last enemy'; and he shared the trials and temptations which are our regular lot and from which or through which we need to be saved.

In underlining this point, the author cannot resist another dig at the angels (v. 16). Jesus did not come to 'help' angels (the author uses a Greek word meaning 'to take the part of'), perhaps because angels, unlike human beings, do not need to be 'saved'. If he had, he would have had to become an angel, but he came down even lower than that, to the level of the 'descendants of Abraham'. The specific mention of Abraham, the ancestor of the Jewish people (and also of the Arabs, but that is presumably not in the author's mind), makes it all the more immediately appropriate to his Jewish readers—and, after all, it was *Jewish* flesh and blood that Jesus shared. But it would be pressing a natural turn of phrase too far to suggest that the author did not also believe that Jesus was the saviour of Gentiles!

The fear of death

An old theological book has the intriguing title *The Death of Death in the Death of Christ*. That seems to be the idea in verses 14–15, but Hebrews is a bit more specific. It is not just 'death' that is destroyed through Jesus' death, but 'the one who has the power of death, the devil', and also 'the fear of death'. There is a limit to the devil's power, of course, but as the one who, through his seduction of Eve, first brought death into the world, and as the one who loves to destroy, the devil stands for death as God stands for life. But the more immediate problem for most people is the 'fear of death'. There is great pastoral realism in the author's observation that people are 'held in slavery' all their lives by this fear. For those who have no hope of life beyond death, this remains the ultimate reality; they cannot see beyond it, and it dominates and ultimately frustrates all their hopes and plans. Life which leads only to death is ultimately pointless. Escape from this 'slavery' is possible only through Christ who has 'brought life and immortality to light through the gospel' (2 Timothy 1:10).

A sacrifice of atonement

If we ask how the death of Christ can have this effect, the author will have a very full answer to offer us later in the letter, but here in verse 17 he gives a brief trailer. This Jesus who shares our human nature is therefore qualified to represent us as our high priest, and it was the role of the priests to offer sacrifices of atonement so that sin might be forgiven. And it is through the forgiveness of sin that we escape death and the fear of death. But why must Jesus *die*? The answer which will be worked out in detail in chapters 7, 9 and 10 is that Jesus is not only priest but also sacrifice, that it was his own blood which he took with him as high priest into the sanctuary to make atonement for the sins of all (9:12). All this remains to be spelled out, but for now at least, a brief note was needed to explain the purpose of the death which is at the heart of Jesus' work as the 'perfect' saviour.

Able to help

It is not only once for all on the cross that Jesus' solidarity with us comes to our aid, but also in our daily trials (v. 18). The English words 'tempt' and 'test' translate the same Greek word, and it is often more appropriate to speak of 'testing' where the traditional English versions speak of 'temptation'. Not only in the wilderness after his baptism, but also throughout his life on earth, Jesus was tested 'in every respect as we are' (4:15). He knows what it is like to be human. When we are up against it, he has been there before us. And so, unlike the angels who have no idea what it is like, he is able to help. We cannot bring to him any problem he has not already faced. He is the perfect saviour.

PRAYER

Help us, Lord, to remember that you have been here before us, and to bring you our troubles with the sure confidence that you can and will bring us safely through. Amen.

The SERVANT & *the* SON

Ask any Jewish schoolboy to name his hero, his favourite character in history, and the chances are he would have named Moses. Moses was, as far as any human being was, the founder of Israel—the man under whose charismatic leadership a rabble of demoralized slaves miraculously escaped from Egypt; the man who took them to the holy mountain where he received from God the laws that were to be the basis of their national life; the man who led them through decades of hardship and danger in the wilderness to within sight of the promised land. All that Israel became as a nation in Canaan, it owed to those early days under Moses.

Moses, therefore, must have an early place in the argument of Hebrews that whatever had been good in the old religion has now been superseded by something better in Christ.

Moses, the servant of God

The Old Testament often describes Moses as God's servant (Exodus 14:31; Numbers 12:8; Joshua 1:2), but he was not just any old servant. Numbers 12:7, quoted here in verse 2, describes him as holding a unique position of trust: whereas prophets heard God's voice only in visions and dreams, Moses, as the faithful overseer of God's household, had direct access to God, 'face to face'.

But he remained a servant (v. 5), and the household (the Greek word means both 'house' and 'household', an ambiguity which our author gladly exploits) over which he had charge was not his household but God's. And his service was not an end in itself, but rather a preparation for 'the things that would be spoken later', when the Son took over the household.

The Son takes precedence

The difference between a servant and a son is that the former will always be looking after someone else's property, while the latter will one day own it. The faithfulness of Moses the servant is not to be compared with the faithfulness of Jesus the Son, for the household over which the Son has authority is, in fact, not only God's household but also his own.

In order to underline this superiority of Jesus, the author picks up the other meaning of 'house'—as a building—and points out in verse 3, rather curiously, that the builder of a house is more important than the house itself. Quite how this observation relates to Moses is not at all clear (he was not a 'building'!) but it is all put into perspective by the further comment that, in the end, all 'building' derives from God the Creator (v. 4). So any credit which a human builder may claim is only relative: all glory belongs ultimately to God. Yet Jesus, the builder of the house, shares that divine glory in a way Moses never could. So the metaphors of household and servant and of house and builder are woven together into a rather awkward demonstration that, for all his importance, Moses remains on the human side of the equation, whereas Jesus, as builder and Son, stands on the side of God.

Following Jesus

So there is no point now in following Moses, the servant, when we are invited rather to belong to Jesus, the Son. In these verses a number of expressions are used to describe how central Jesus' role now is in the plan of salvation. He is our 'apostle' (v. 1), the one sent by God to call people into his new household. He is the 'high priest of our confession' ('of the religion we profess', NEB); Moses had shared his leadership with Aaron, the high priest, but Jesus combines the roles of both, as we will discover more fully in chapters 5—7. And he is both the builder of the house and the faithful ruler of the household, so that a Christian is a member not just of God's household, but also, more specifically, of the household of Jesus.

Our author is not going to let slip an opportunity to reinforce the appeal to his readers which he began in 2:1–4. There is a warning as well as an encouragement in the words 'if we hold firm' (v. 6), for it was just that 'holding firm' which was in doubt. This is the concern which he will develop in the verses that follow. But let us notice here what it is that should characterize the faithful Christian: 'the confidence and the pride that belong to our hope' (and compare verse 1, 'holy partners in a heavenly calling'). Those words are worth pondering: is that how you would define Christianity?

FOR REFLECTION

Think through what you know of the story of Moses, and consider how Jesus compares to him. Does the 'servant' and 'Son' contrast ring true?

57 HEBREWS 3:7–13

The IMPORTANCE *of* 'TODAY'

The warning slipped in at the end of verse 6 is now developed into a full-scale pastoral exhortation which will go on right down to 4:13. It is the second of the 'expositions' of Old Testament texts which we noted in Study 44 as a characteristic of this author's writing, and this one is a lot longer and more elaborately worked out than the exposition of Psalm 8 in chapter 2.

The message of Psalm 95

The text of this 'sermon' is set out in full in verses 7–11. It is the second half of Psalm 95, a psalm better known to Anglicans as the *Venite*, set in the Prayer Book for daily use at Morning Prayer. But it is interesting to observe that the part of the psalm which our author chooses for his sermon is the part Anglicans have traditionally been less keen on. In many churches where the old Prayer Book remains in use, only the first seven verses of the *Venite* are used, leaving out precisely the bit that Hebrews focuses on. And the more modern *Alternative Service Book* has a truncated version of Psalm 95 which peters out at the beginning of verse 8 and concludes rather lamely with some words drawn from Psalm 96 in place of the section which we are now to study. Clearly the message of Psalm 95 which the author of Hebrews felt to be important is one which modern Anglicans find embarrassing!

The second half of the psalm is a solemn warning not to ignore God's voice. It is based on the experience of Israel in the wilderness under Moses' leadership. (Is that why it came to mind at this point, just after the author has discussed Moses' faithfulness?) Unlike Moses, the Israelites 'hardened their hearts', and despite all that God continued to do for them they turned against him and his servant Moses. The specific incident that is referred to in verses 8 and 9 is in Exodus 17:1–7, where the Israelites' lack of water caused them to demand a miracle to prove that God really was with them. Moses 'called the place Massah and Meribah (testing and strife) because the Israelites quarrelled and tested the Lord, saying "Is the Lord among us or not?"' This and many other such incidents culminated in their refusal to go in and fight for the promised land, so that God condemned them instead to wander in the desert until all that generation had died. So they failed to 'enter God's rest' in the promised land.

Psalm 95 applied

In Hebrews 3:7—4:13 our author will constantly return to these verses of Psalm 95, and will explore their significance from a number of angles, particularly the theme of rest in the promised land. But the main point of his quotation is to draw attention simply to the exhortation, 'Today, if you hear his voice, do not harden your hearts'. It is clearly something he can all too easily envisage his readers doing, and in verses 12–13 he spells out the danger.

He warns them against, literally, 'a bad heart of unbelief', and defines this danger more specifically as the tendency to 'turn away from the living God'. While the phrase 'the living God' does not occur very frequently in the Bible, when it does occur it is to be noticed, and four of those occurrences are in Hebrews (3:12; 9:14; 10:31; 12:22). It contrasts the deadness of a religion of mere ritual with the service of an active, personal God, who invites his people to know him personally, not just to keep a code of laws, and who is not to be trifled with. To turn away from such a God is to abandon true religion altogether. Only 'the deceitfulness of sin' could prevail on those who have known true faith to make such a disastrous move.

'Today'

The 'today' of the psalmist was long after the days of Moses. For our author it has not yet passed. It is still 'today', and the voice of God is still there to be heard. But the psalm suggests that 'today' does not last for ever. There is also a 'too late' in the purposes of God. So the matter is urgent. They must 'exhort one another every day, as long as it is called "today"' (v. 13). It is a matter of life and death.

PRAYER

Living God, let me hear your voice today; and when I hear it, may my heart not be hard. Amen.

Failure *in the* Wilderness

The exposition of Psalm 95:7–11 now gets under way in more detail, as the author explains the historical references to the wilderness experiences of Israel, and begins to point out the relevance of those ancient stories to his readers' own contemporary situation.

(I have divided the text into daily portions for convenience, but the exposition flows unbroken from 3:7 to 4:13, and each section builds on what has gone before.)

Those who failed

In verse 15, the author again picks up the key verse on which this 'sermon' is based—the appeal not to neglect God's voice when it is heard—but he extends it to include the phrase 'as in the rebellion', because this phrase establishes the historical reference that is the basis of the psalm's appeal. It is this historical reference that he first needs to explain, and he does so by means of a series of questions and answers in verses 16–18.

The three questions and their answers all, in effect, point to the same group of people, the Israelites who left Egypt under Moses. For it was that whole generation who turned against Moses and, frightened by the reports of the gigantic inhabitants, refused God's call to go in and take possession of Canaan. The turning point is recorded in chapters 13 and 14 of Numbers, and it is in God's angry response to his people's faithlessness in Numbers 14:26–35 that we find the verdict, which Hebrews here echoes, that their dead bodies would fall in the wilderness, and that not one of those who came out of Egypt as adults would live to see the eventual conquest of the promised land—with two noble exceptions. At the end of forty years of wandering in the wilderness, the only men who would still be alive to enter Canaan would be Caleb and Joshua, the two men of faith included in the reconnaissance mission whose 'minority report' concluded that God was well able to bring them safely into the land. They were overruled at the time, but they had been right, and only they would live to see their prediction come true.

So the fundamental problem which led to Israel's failure in the wilderness was 'unbelief' (v. 19). Caleb and Joshua saw the same formidable opponents as the other spies, but they were able to see beyond the problem to the power of God to solve it. That was their 'faith', the sort of faith which the author of Hebrews will celebrate much more fully in chapter 11, the 'conviction of things not seen'. For the rest, despite their experience of miraculous deliverance from Egypt, the problem of Canaanite power loomed larger than trust in God, and this 'unbelief' led them into 'disobedience' to the divine calling. That was why God was angry, and swore that they should never reach the 'rest' of the promised land. So 'they were unable to enter because of unbelief'.

Learning from the past

The readers of this letter have also received 'good news', just as the Israelites received the good news from Caleb and Joshua (4:2). But good news is only effective if it is taken up and acted on—it requires the response of faith. And that, the author fears, is their problem. They are indeed 'partners of Christ' (3:14), just as the Israelites had been partners of Moses, but they could not presume on being saved by association any more than the rebellious Israelites. Their own faith must be secure.

So they must 'hold their first confidence firm to the end' (3:14), and not 'drift away' into unbelief. The promise of rest remains open for them (4:1), but it remains possible that they, like the Israelites, will fail to achieve it. Psalm 95 has set before them an awesome reminder of the danger of not responding to the voice of God. They must not allow history to repeat itself.

FOR REFLECTION

If you have time, read chapters 13 and 14 of Numbers. (Reading Hebrews constantly forces us back to the Old Testament, and I hope you will take the opportunity to refresh your memory of the passages the author refers to.)

Can you think of any situations today which might offer a parallel to the story of the spies and Israel's disobedience? What would the author of Hebrews have to say about them?

59 HEBREWS 4:3–10

GOD'S REST—*and* OURS

The exposition of Psalm 95 continues, and the central exhortation, 'Today, if you hear his voice, do not harden your hearts' is repeated again in verse 7. But while that remains the main point of our author's use of Psalm 95, the word with which that psalm concludes offers a further theme to explore, the theme of 'rest'. The danger is that by failing to respond to God's voice, his readers may fail to reach their 'rest'; but what sort of 'rest' is it which is held out before them as their ultimate goal? The 'rest' to which the psalm refers was a historical situation of long ago, the entry to the promised land of Canaan. That is no longer an issue. So what other 'rest', what 'promised land', still remains open for the people of God?

The seventh day

The 'rest' which the Israelites failed to enter because of their unbelief is described by God in Psalm 95:11 as '*my* rest'. That could mean simply 'the rest which I give, to which I am calling them', but the personal pronoun also suggests a further thought. What is 'God's rest'? And the answer is obvious to any Jew—the sabbath.

Rest is what follows from labour, and at the end of the labour of creation, 'God rested on the seventh day from all the work that he had done' (Genesis 2:2). Here is the supreme paradigm of rest: all is completed and achieved, and there remains nothing further but to rest in the enjoyment of all that has been done.

So it is also for God's people. When their work is done, they too may look forward to 'ceasing from their labours' as God did (v. 10). The author does not spell out here just what we may expect that ultimate sabbath 'rest' to be like, but later in the letter he will paint an attractive picture of heaven as the place of final security and enjoyment (11:13–16; 12:22–23), and it seems likely that he has heaven in view here as the 'promised land' at the end of our earthly pilgrimage. There God's people will share his own rest.

So that is the 'rest' which still 'remains open' (v. 6), but which, no less than the 'rest' of Canaan, will not come automatically. It must be 'entered', and it can be forfeited through disobedience stemming from unbelief. So the stakes are high, and the appeal not to harden your hearts when you hear the voice of God achieves fresh urgency. For the Israelites in the wilderness, the prize was the peaceful enjoyment of an earthly kingdom, but for these Hebrew Christians it is nothing less than the eternal sharing of God's perpetual sabbath rest, the hope of heaven.

Joshua and Jesus

The main theme of this part of the exposition of Psalm 95 is the nature of the 'rest' to be won, but in explaining that the Christian 'rest' is something different from the conquest of Canaan, our author refers in passing to the man under whose leadership that original 'rest' was eventually to be found, Joshua the son of Nun (v. 8), one of the two spies who maintained their faith in God's promise, and were rewarded with entry to the promised land. Here is another of the great heroes of Israel—Moses' chosen successor, and the man who was privileged to enjoy what even Moses himself was denied; the warrior hero of Jericho and many other great battles; the man under whose leadership the covenant of God with his people was finally established within the land of Canaan. If Moses was the Jewish schoolboy's favourite hero, Joshua must have come a close second.

So he too comes in for comparison with Jesus, a comparison which is the more fascinating in that their names are the same. ('Jesus' is the Greek form of the Hebrew name Joshua, so that verse 8 in Greek begins 'If *Jesus* had given them rest', and only the context tells you that this was the ancient 'Jesus', not his recent counterpart.) But again, of course, the comparison is in fact a contrast. Joshua could not have given them real 'rest'; otherwise, why should Psalm 95 speak of a 'rest' still to be achieved? It is only in the second Joshua that real 'rest' can be found, the sabbath rest of the people of God (v. 9).

FOR REFLECTION

O what their joy and their glory must be,
Those endless sabbaths the blessed ones see!
Crown for the valiant; to weary ones rest;
God shall be all, and in all ever blest.

Peter Abelard (1079–1143), translated by John Mason Neale

60 HEBREWS 4:11–13

The SWORD *of* GOD

As the exposition of Psalm 95:7–11 comes to an end, we find in these verses first a general summary of the message which Hebrews has drawn from the psalm, and then a memorable concluding comment on the power of the word of God, which serves as a further warning not to take lightly the exhortation based on that psalm.

Final exhortation

The call to 'make every effort' (v. 11) could also be translated 'be zealous' or 'eager'. It is a matter of attitude as well as of activity. The author of Hebrews wants his readers to be in no doubt that this matter of 'entering rest' must be their single most important concern. All other considerations must give way before this spiritual imperative. For if that 'rest' is lost, everything else is lost as well.

Their situation is not the same as that of the Israelites under Moses, but the disobedience which cost them the promised land may have its counterpart in other situations. If the Israelites in the wilderness could miss their goal by turning back and refusing to march on in faith, so could these Hebrew Christians if they were to turn back from their commitment to Christ. And the very urgency of the author's warning makes it clear that he believed that this was a real possibility.

We shall return to this question especially in relation to 6:4–6 and 10:26–31. Some interpreters have argued on theological grounds that it is impossible for a Christian, once saved, to be lost. That may be good theology, but it does not seem to match up to experience, and it is clear that our author can envisage ultimate apostasy and the loss of salvation as a real danger to these Christian people. Their faith in Christ means that they are on the road to heaven, but it is still possible to 'fall' and to lose the prize.

The penetrating word of God

That is why God has spoken. He spoke to the Israelites in the wilderness, by an oath (Psalm 95:11), and they were not able to escape that oath. And he has further spoken through the words of Psalm 95, which the writer has been so powerfully deploying in the preceding verses. This 'word of God' is not just a dead letter of the past, but, as the word of the 'living God' (3:12), it is itself alive and active, and cannot be evaded.

Such language echoes Old Testament statements about how God's word springs into action. God sends out his word and it 'runs swiftly' in the world, affecting both the natural creation and human affairs (Psalm 147:15–20). It goes out from God's mouth and accomplishes the purpose for which he has sent it (Isaiah 55:11). It is like a fire, and a hammer which breaks up the rocks (Jeremiah 23:29). This dynamic understanding of the word of God is vividly symbolized in the picture of a 'sharp, two-edged sword' coming out of the mouth of the risen Lord in Revelation 1:16.

So too here the author pictures the word of God as sharper even than a two-edged sword. (Is he thinking of Numbers 14:43, where even after God's oath some Israelites none the less tried to enter Canaan directly, only to be cut down by the sword of the Amalekites and Canaanites? God's word is sharper even than that.) As such it can penetrate to the depths of our being, and to the secret thoughts of our hearts. So we cannot hide from God (v. 13). When such a God speaks, it would be folly not to listen. They would not get away with it, any more than ancient Israel did.

The author does not spell out where we may expect to hear the word of God. Presumably he is thinking here at least of Psalm 95 and its message. But he hardly needs to spell it out, because it is clear from nearly every line of his letter where he himself looks for the 'word of God'—the Old Testament. In those pages is all that they need to know the mind of God and to respond to his demands. But it is quite likely that he also has in mind the 'word' as it now comes through Christian preachers (of whom surely he himself was one), the word which for us now is brought together in the New Testament.

Whenever and however we hear God's voice, we cannot afford to 'harden our hearts'. We will not get away with it.

PRAYER

Thank you, Lord, that you have spoken—through your prophets and sacred writings, and now also through your Son. As your word penetrates into our lives and hearts, may we not resist it, but respond in faith and obedience. Amen.

61 HEBREWS 4:14–16

CHRISTIAN CONFIDENCE

In 3:1 the author referred to Jesus as 'the high priest of our confession', but did not stop at that time to explain what he meant. Now he reintroduces the theme, and this time it will be at the centre of his argument for a substantial section of the letter which stretches from 4:14 to the end of chapter 7, and will undergird his whole discussion of sacrificial ritual in chapters 8—10.

Approaching the throne of grace

From 5:1 on he will begin to explain the matter in detail, but first in these verses we have a broad and heart-warming statement of what it means to have Jesus as our high priest. It is focused on the theme of access to God.

The role of a priest in the Old Testament was partly to represent God to his people, through teaching his law, but also, and mainly, to represent the people before God. The priest offered on the people's behalf the sacrifices which they were not entitled to offer for themselves. He was an intermediary between the people and their God; it was through his work that they had access to God.

The effect of having Jesus as our high priest is that we can now ourselves 'approach the throne of grace with boldness'. He has opened the way for us, a 'new and living way' (10:20), and through him we can come to God with no other intermediary needed.

A high priest in heaven

Unlike the Old Testament priests, who were mere earthbound human beings like ourselves, Jesus our new high priest has 'passed through the heavens' (v. 14). 'Passing through' sounds odd, and seems to suggest that he was on his way to somewhere else! But it is the language of priesthood, of the chief priest in Old Testament times who once a year 'passed through' the veil into the inner sanctuary of the temple to represent the people before God. This ceremony is important to the argument of Hebrews about Jesus' priesthood, and the author will several times return to the theme: the sanctuary into which Jesus has entered is not on earth but in heaven, the true and abiding sanctuary of the presence of God himself (6:19–20; 8:1–2;

9:11–12, 24; 10:11–13). So he has 'passed through' the heavenly realms to the very throne of God, and there he stands as our representative. Moreover, he is himself the Son of God; we could not have better representation!

A high priest who understands

And yet there is another equally important but contrasting point. Verse 15 returns to the theme of 2:18, Jesus' solidarity with us. This high priest is not a remote figure, but one of us. He knows by experience what human weakness is like. He understands our problems, because they have also been his. Of course this was true also of the Old Testament priests, but there is a crucial difference: they, being human, not only experienced temptation but also succumbed to it. So, as 5:3 will remind us, they had to offer sacrifices for their own sins as well. Jesus has no such handicap; he is 'without sin', and so he alone can offer the perfect sacrifice.

Verses 14 and 15 thus represent the two essential qualifications of our high priest. He is the Son of God in heaven; but he is also one of us, and knows for himself the weaknesses of earthly life. Take away either truth, and you have a figure who is either remote or ineffective; only if both are true do you have the perfect saviour.

Boldness before God

With such a representative, we have nothing to fear. We may confidently 'hold fast our confession' and approach God's throne 'with boldness' (v. 16). And at God's throne there is 'mercy' and 'grace to help'. This idea of Christ's high priesthood is no merely intellectual concept; it is the basis of our spiritual security. To this truth we may boldly turn 'in time of need', and we will not be let down.

FOR REFLECTION

Reflect on the two complementary truths about Jesus, our high priest, in verses 14 and 15. A modern theologian has claimed that you can have the humanity without the divinity, or the divinity without the humanity, but 'there is absolutely no way of having both'. How do you think our author would have answered him?

HEBREWS 5:1–6

QUALIFICATIONS *for* PRIESTHOOD

During his time on earth Jesus was not a priest—he was not born into the right family (a point Hebrews will take up in 7:11–19). So the author now has to justify his claim that the risen Jesus may rightly be described as our 'high priest'. In these verses he looks at two essential qualifications for priesthood—real humanity (vv. 1–3) and a divine appointment (vv. 4–6).

The priest as a human representative

It may seem strange to insist that priests must be human—what other sort might there be? But we have already seen in 2:10–18 and in 4:15–16 how important this theme of the real humanity of Jesus is for the argument of Hebrews. There has often been a tendency among Christians so to emphasize Christ's divinity that he seems to be scarcely human at all, but that would undermine the essential solidarity of Jesus with his people, and without that solidarity there is no salvation.

So in verses 1–3 we are reminded that human solidarity is an essential qualification for priesthood. In these verses this is merely stated as a known and obvious fact; it will not be until verses 7–10 that he explains how this observation relates specifically to Jesus.

So the (Old Testament) high priest, chosen from among human beings, is in a position to carry out his ministry on behalf of human beings (the word is repeated in Greek), as their representative before God. And because he shares the same human weaknesses, he can understand and sympathize with those he represents. When we talk of the priest offering sacrifices *on behalf of* other people, this does not imply that he himself has no need of spiritual help. His sacrifices are for himself as well as for others.

This is a perspective which is surely important to keep in mind in relation to Christian pastoral ministry today: any ministry which puts the minister on a pedestal above the people is hypocritical; he or she is also a sinner like them. But here, of course, is one of the areas where Jesus' priesthood is different and 'better', as we shall see in 7:26–28. He shares our humanity, but not our sin, and so only he has no need to offer a sacrifice for himself.

The priest called by God

In the Old Testament, no one could decide for themselves to be a priest. God chose Aaron and his family, and it was only those born into that family who could be priests. But Jesus was not of the family of Aaron, so what is the basis of his calling to be our high priest? True to form, our author finds the answer in two quotations from the Old Testament, both from psalms which we have already met in this letter.

The first is Psalm 2:7, already quoted in 1:5. It does not relate directly to priesthood, but to the higher title of 'Son of God'. Jesus owes this title not to his own choice but to God, who has declared him to be his Son.

The other quotation is from Psalm 110 (see comments on 1:3 and 1:13), not now its first verse about sitting at God's right hand, but verse 4 about being a 'priest for ever'—a status which the first part of the verse attributes to God's oath: 'The Lord has sworn and will not change his mind'. (The author will develop this point in 7:20–22.) So Jesus' priestly status derives from God's appointment.

But Psalm 110:4 has also introduced another vital piece in the jigsaw, the 'order of Melchizedek'. This, as we shall see (7:11–19), is the basis on which the author of Hebrews can argue for Jesus' priesthood even though he was not from the family of Aaron, for Psalm 110 (uniquely in the Old Testament) envisages a second (and, as the author will demonstrate, a superior) order of priesthood—that of Melchizedek. It is this radical concept which he will explore with such diligence in chapter 7, and we must wait until then to follow his argument. But already he has put his chief card on the table. Jesus is a priest indeed, appointed as such by God, but a priest of a different kind and, unlike the Aaronic priests, 'for ever' (v. 6).

PRAYER

Lord Jesus, Son of God and our high priest, thank you that you can sympathize with our human weakness. May we, through you, approach the throne of grace with boldness, and find grace to help in time of need. Amen.

63 HEBREWS 5:7–10

PERFECT *through* SUFFERING

In Study 54 we first came across the idea of Jesus needing to be 'made perfect' in order to be our saviour. In these verses the theme is more fully developed. As we noted then, 'perfect' is used here not in the sense of *moral* perfection or sinlessness, but of being 'fully qualified' to carry out the role assigned to him, that of saviour for humanity.

Sharing our lot

We return now to the first qualification for priesthood set out in 5:1–3, the need for a priest to represent his people by being thoroughly one of them, and thus sympathizing with their human weakness. Jesus amply fulfilled this requirement 'in the days of his flesh' (v. 7). That phrase shows that the author understands clearly that the period of Jesus' incarnation was only a part of the whole story, preceded by his eternal existence as the Son of God through whom the worlds were made (1:2–12), and followed by the present time when the risen and ascended Lord has 'passed through the heavens' (4:14). The 'days of his flesh' were that temporary period during which, in order to fulfil his role as our saviour, he became 'for a little while lower than the angels' (2:9).

The letter to the Hebrews is remarkable for its ability to hold side by side the most exalted concept of Jesus' eternal divinity and glory with the most earthy realism concerning his human experience. There is nothing merely skin-deep about his humanity. There are, of course, plenty of accounts in the Gospels of Jesus praying, but the very strong language about 'prayers and supplications, with loud cries and tears' suggests that the author is thinking especially of his long and agonized prayer in Gethsemane that the cup might pass. That was precisely a prayer to 'the one who was able to save him from death', and that was what he prayed for.

But that prayer was not granted: Jesus still went to the cross, fully persuaded that this was his Father's will. So what does the author mean by saying that 'he was heard because of his reverent submission'? 'Reverent submission' there was indeed, as Jesus concluded, 'Yet, not what I want, but what you want' (Mark 14:36), and it was that second part of his prayer, not the first, which 'was heard'. The fear of death, which was real and painful and which Jesus shares with the rest of us

(2:15), was thus overcome, and his death proved to be for him but the prelude to resurrection and glory. He has been through the 'valley of the shadow of death', and has come out victorious. In that way, though not in the specific request for the cup to pass, he 'was heard'.

Learning obedience

Again, the phrase is open to misunderstanding. It may seem to suggest that Jesus was previously disobedient, but was 'brought to heel' through his sufferings. But that is not the point. He was the Son of God, and for the Son of God the acceptance of death in obedience to his Father's will was a new and profoundly disturbing experience. Thus he 'learned obedience' (v. 8) in the sense that he tasted this unfamiliar experience. And thus it is through that suffering of death, deeply feared but then obediently accepted, that he has become 'perfect', fully equipped to be the saviour of those whose life is likewise characterized by loud cries and tears and the fear of death.

Jesus, the Son, is therefore now, as a result of his experience of suffering and obedience, in a position to bring to his people not salvation from (physical) death, which we, like him, must experience, but an 'eternal salvation' (v. 9) which takes away the sting of death. It remains to explore just how that salvation is achieved, and by another reference to Psalm 110:4 ('a high priest according to the order of Melchizedek') our author signals how that argument is going to be developed. Its development will be delayed by what seems something of a digression in 5:11—6:20, but then in 6:20 a further reference to Psalm 110:4 will launch us into the full account of Jesus' high priestly ministry in chapter 7.

PRAYER

Thanks be to thee, O Lord Jesus Christ,
for all the benefits thou hast won for us;
for all the pains and insults thou hast borne for us.
O most merciful redeemer, Friend and Brother,
may we know thee more clearly,
love thee more dearly,
and follow thee more nearly. Amen.

Richard, Bishop of Chichester, 13th century

64 HEBREWS 5:11—6:3

TIME *to* GROW UP

At this point, the author breaks off to express his frustration about his readers' failure to understand. Clearly he knows the group to whom he is writing well enough to realize that as his argument becomes more complicated, and especially now as he wants to begin to unpack the significance of 'the order of Melchizedek', he is likely to leave them behind. He would like to share some solid food with them, but they still need milk. It seems, however, that in the end he will decide to press on regardless with the explanation of Melchizedek in chapter 7—or if the Melchizedek argument is still 'milk', we may well wonder what solid food would be like!

Infancy and maturity

Maturity in Christian discipleship and understanding does not come automatically with the passing of years. These Hebrew Christians have been following Jesus for some time, long enough for them to have had time to grasp the faith firmly enough to be able to teach others as well. But our author knows better. What he has heard of their present spiritual instability suggests to him that they have not yet assimilated even the basic elements of Christian faith. They are still infants, in need of the most elementary teaching (milk).

The word for 'the mature' in 5:14 belongs to the same group as the various 'perfection' words we have already noted—and the 'perfection' to which he calls his readers in 6:1 is the same concept. Again the issue is not moral rectitude, but full development. A 'mature' Christian is one who is 'skilled in the word of righteousness' (5:13), 'whose faculties have been trained [the word refers literally to physical exercise] by practice to distinguish good from evil'. 'Adult' Christians are those who can make responsible decisions for themselves, based on their knowledge of God's word, and do not need to be told by others what they should do and think. It is such people who are able to teach others. But so far these Hebrew Christians have lamentably failed to grow up.

So in 6:1–3 he appeals to them to move on to maturity. When foundations have been well laid, they do not need to be revisited. There are basic truths which we ought to be able to take for granted, so that we may move on to deeper understanding.

On not going back to square one

So six elementary matters are listed in 6:1–2, so briefly that they leave us with some question marks. They read rather surprisingly as a list of Christian basics. They may conveniently be considered in pairs.

The first two are clear enough: repentance and faith are often mentioned in the New Testament as the essence of Christian conversion; the specific mention of repentance from 'dead works' (rather than a more general term like 'sin') is particularly appropriate to conversion from a formal Jewish religion to living faith, as the author will explain in 9:11–14.

A mention of Christian baptism would follow naturally, but 'baptisms' is plural, and the word used is not the normal term for Christian baptism but one which elsewhere refers to Jewish purification rites (as in 9:10) and might better be translated 'ablutions'. Together with 'laying on of hands' (used in the Old Testament for commissioning people for office and in connection with sacrifices), it seems to take us back into Jewish ritual rather than specifically Christian faith. The early instruction of these Jewish Christians apparently had started from their Old Testament roots, though we may assume that the 'instruction' on these matters included a contrast between the former ablutions and Christian baptism.

Similarly 'the resurrection of the dead' (not specifically the resurrection of Jesus) and 'eternal judgment' were matters of Jewish belief, though with the coming of Jesus each took on a crucial new dimension.

So the six 'basic elements' prove to be a curious mixture of the Jewish and the Christian, reflecting the early stages of progress from Judaism into Christianity. That is where these people still are, after all these years. It is time for them to move on into a more distinctively Christian understanding, and that is what our author now wants to help them with, if only they are willing to grow up.

FOR REFLECTION

If you were drawing up a list of half a dozen 'Christian basics', what would they be? Why do you think the list given in these verses is different (if it is)?

65 HEBREWS 6:4–8

The DANGER *of* APOSTASY

A threat to Christian assurance?

These verses, with 10:26–31, are among the most uncomfortable in the New Testament. They appear to say that those who have begun on the Christian path will not necessarily reach the end of it, that it is possible for a former believer to be finally lost. They thus form a sharp contrast with passages such as John 10:27–29 which assure us that Christ's sheep can never be snatched from his hand, and with much of the theology of Paul which insists that those whom God has called he will bring safe to glory (such as Romans 8:28–39).

A popular way to resolve this problem has been to argue that the people described in these verses were never really true Christians at all, that their 'taste' of God's good gifts was merely a superficial interest which was never translated into the commitment of Christian faith. We shall see that the terms our author uses in these verses do not encourage this suggestion. More importantly, these verses, in the context in which we find them, do not read like a merely academic discussion. It is the author's own intended readers whom he is warning in the sternest terms of the danger they are in. And yet there is no doubt that he is writing to them as real Christians, not as interested onlookers. He is not saying that they have yet reached the point of no return (6:9), but he is afraid that they may. What he is holding out to them is not a hypothetical case which could never really happen—why should he? He is warning them to turn back from the brink.

Resolving the tension

Must we then settle for a theological contradiction between Hebrews on the one hand and Paul and John on the other? It is certainly hard to find a neat logical pattern which allows room both for ultimate security and for ultimate apostasy. But perhaps that is to come at the question the wrong way. We may do better to think about the purposes for which these contrasting passages were written.

There are Christians who are plagued by doubt and fear, and find it hard to relax in the confidence that God is in ultimate control, that 'underneath are the everlasting arms'. For them the assurance of John

10:27–29 and Romans 8:28–39 is the most important teaching that could be given. It is support for the faint-hearted.

But there are others whose danger is not doubt but complacency. An arrogant assumption that all is well, coupled with a disregard for God's word, is a dangerous cocktail. People who are drifting into such an attitude need to be pulled up sharp, and Hebrews 6:4–8 is such a pastoral warning. It is a shot across the bows of the careless.

No going back

In any other context no one would doubt that the experiences described in verses 4 and 5 (enlightenment, God's 'heavenly gift', participation in the Holy Spirit, experience of God's word and of supernatural power) are those of true Christian conversion. 'Tasting' is used not as a contrast with really eating, but as a mark of actual experience rather than theoretical knowledge (as in Psalm 34:8).

Such experience changes a person for ever, and cannot be cancelled out. You cannot revert to a non-Christian state as if nothing had happened. To 'fall away' after such a conversion is to 'recrucify the Son of God' (v. 6) and someone who has done that cannot then turn round and say they didn't mean it. It is not that someone else has 'snatched them from Christ's hand'—they have done it themselves, and in so doing have placed themselves beyond help. It is 'impossible to restore them to repentance' (v. 4). They are no longer worth cultivating (vv. 7–8). It is not a matter of what God *can* do, so much as what he *will* do: there can come a point where he will not interfere with a deliberate human decision. Such an open-eyed reversal, like the 'unforgivable sin' of Mark 3:28–30, is terminal.

FOR REFLECTION

I have suggested that the tension between ultimate security and ultimate apostasy may be understood not so much by logically squaring the circle, as by recognizing different pastoral needs. Do you agree? Can you think of people or circumstances for which the different approaches of John 10:27–29 and of Hebrews 6:4–8 would be appropriate?

After the STICK, *the* CARROT

It is as if, having launched his torpedo in 6:4–8, the author is afraid that he may have expressed himself too directly, and now enters on a damage limitation exercise. While he meant what he said in the preceding verses (as 10:26–31 will show), he does not want his readers to think that he has actually written them off. He has pointed out in no uncertain terms the danger of the course they may have been contemplating, but he did so only in order to keep them from it, and now (and through the rest of this chapter) he redresses the balance by expressing his confidence in them and appealing to their sense of Christian commitment.

'God is not unjust'

The very solemn possibility contemplated in 6:4–8 must not be taken to suggest that God *wants* anyone to be lost. God, who knows everything about them (4:12–13), is well aware that, however strong the pressure, they have not yet succumbed to it. Verse 10 indicates a long and honourable record of genuine Christian service, and that service has been directed specifically towards other Christian people ('the saints') when they were in trouble, as we shall learn more fully in 10:32–34. Such behaviour is a clear sign of their sincere Christian faith, and God will not overlook it. No one who serves God will finish up the loser.

So they have nothing to fear, so long as they remain on the course they are now following, the course of faithful Christian discipleship. For all his warnings about what *might* happen, the author does not really expect it in their case. He is writing the letter to help to prevent such a disaster, and he is confident that they will respond in the right way. As a good pastor, he knows the value of encouragement and of affirmation.

Keeping going to the end

The appeal to 'each one of you' (v. 11) shows that, while he is writing to the group as a corporate whole, it was possible that some might break ranks. In 10:24–25 he will return to this fear, and will urge them to have a concern for one another and to find strength in their fellowship, and again in 12:15–17 he warns against the possibility of some individual going the wrong way and affecting others in the group. As in Paul's image of the Church as a body in which each part depends on and has a responsibility towards the others, the health of the Christian community depends on the spiritual health of each of its members.

Verses 11–12 contain several of the terms typical of the author's appeal to his readers throughout the letter—'diligence', 'full assurance', 'faith', 'patience', 'to the very end'. This theme will come to a climax in his great account of 'faith' in chapter 11, and in that chapter we shall see how the essence of a persevering faith is the conviction that God's promises will be fulfilled. That is the basis of the 'hope' to which he calls them here, because the fulfilment of the Christian hope is in the eventual inheriting of what God has promised. Christian discipleship is not a blind loyalty which grits its teeth and presses on just for the sake of it. It is a clear-sighted pursuit of a goal, and that goal is determined not by human wishful thinking, but by the declared purpose of God for his people, the promise of a heavenly reward which will put all the earthly troubles in perspective. It is that positive vision, as well as the negative fear of ultimate loss, which is to motivate these Hebrew Christians as they continue to resist temptation and to press on in loyalty to the Christian hope set before them.

The alternative is to become 'sluggish' (v. 12), like a lazy and careless worker who leaves a job half done. Like the language of 'drifting away' in 2:1, this suggests that their danger was not only of a deliberate and decisive *volte face*, but also of the slow attrition of their Christian commitment by sheer lack of attention and determination. That is why this letter is needed, to wake them up before it is too late.

PRAYER

Thank you, Lord, for the hope you have set before us in our Christian faith. Help us to keep our sights on the goal, and not to become 'sluggish'. Amen.

67 HEBREWS 6:13–20

The ANCHOR *of the* SOUL

The mention of God's promises (6:12) leads the author to explain the basis of our confidence that God will do as he has said, a confidence of which Abraham offers a prime example which will be more fully developed in 11:8–19.

God's oath

An oath (usually using the name of God) is the way we show that we really mean what we say, and that it can be relied on (v. 16). Since God has no one greater by whom he can swear, he confirms his promises by swearing 'by himself' (v. 13). The phrase is drawn from Genesis 22:16, 'By myself I have sworn, says the Lord', and the promise that followed in Genesis 22:17–18 was the basis of Abraham's hope and the foundation of Israel's national identity. If we can trust what God says, how much more when he confirms it with an oath.

Most commentators understand the 'two unchangeable things' of verse 18 as God's promise and his oath, and that is probably right. But it may also be worth remembering that the oath quoted in verses 13–14, the promise to Abraham, is not the only oath of God which our author is thinking about, and in verse 20 we are reminded again of God's oath to the Messiah that he would be a priest for ever. In 7:20–22 he will make the point explicitly that this declaration was confirmed by God's oath, and it is this promise, rather than the promise to Abraham, which is at the heart of the letter's argument and is the basis of the 'hope set before us' (v. 18), when we acknowledge Jesus as our high priest. It is possible, therefore, that the two unchangeable things he refers to are the *two* divine oaths of Genesis 22:16–18 and of Psalm 110:4.

Taking God at his word

Since God cannot lie, his oath and promise give us an absolutely secure basis for our Christian hope. The imagery of 'taking refuge' is vividly explained by F.F. Bruce as follows: 'We are refugees from the sinking ship of the present world-order, so soon to disappear.' The metaphors pile up in rich confusion in verses 18–20: we are refugees who have 'seized' the hope; this hope is an immovable anchor, and yet has 'entered the inner shrine behind the curtain' of the tabernacle, where the ark of God was found, the holiest place of all; and in that holy place is Jesus, our high priest, who has gone ahead and made his way through the curtain as our forerunner. Metaphors are metaphors, and need not be pressed into logical consistency. The whole complex of ideas is one of ultimate security, of the most powerful reassurance to those who might be tempted to doubt whether it was all worthwhile, whether God really could be trusted to fulfil his promises.

So the anchor is 'hope'. The word 'hope' generally suggests something not yet assured: to hope for something is less than to be sure of it. But not in the New Testament. There 'hope' stands for that ultimate reality towards which we are travelling and of which, as this passage so strongly insists, we may be absolutely sure—as sure as God is sure. It is that hope which is the foundation of the faith and perseverance the writer is calling for, for 'faith is the assurance of things hoped for' (11:1), and such assurance cannot be disappointed when the hope rests on the oath and the promise of God.

High priest and forerunner

So we have come back in verse 20 to the theme of Jesus the high priest. The high priest is pictured here in his climactic annual role on the Day of Atonement when he went through the curtain into the inner sanctuary bearing the sacrifice of atonement for the sins of the people. But now there is no need of an annual ceremony: Jesus is there in the sanctuary for ever. And whereas in the Old Testament ritual no one else was allowed to go through the curtain, Jesus has gone in as 'forerunner on our behalf', which seems to imply that now we may follow. Is that too daring an idea? No, for the author will develop it in just that way in 10:19–20. The way is now open. That is what it meant when the curtain of the temple was torn apart as Jesus died on the cross (Mark 15:38).

FOR REFLECTION

Some people say that for Christians to claim 'assurance of salvation' is arrogant. How do you think the author of Hebrews would have responded?

Enter Melchizedek

Who is Melchizedek?

The mysterious figure of Melchizedek appears only three times in the Bible—Genesis 14:18–20; Psalm 110:4; and here in Hebrews. Later Jewish interpreters found him intriguing, and various speculations took him to be a messianic or angelic figure. It is Psalm 110:4 which has drawn our author's attention to him, because it speaks of an order of priesthood different from (and older than) the official Aaronic priests of the Old Testament law.

Moreover, Psalm 110, which our author has already drawn on, is almost unique in the Old Testament in that it speaks of a figure who is at the same time king (sitting at God's right hand) and priest. Usually in the Old Testament the two offices were kept strictly separate: kings could not be priests and priests could not be kings. So in Melchizedek there is a rare precedent for a quite new type of royal priesthood.

And to add yet more to the interest of this ancient character, he was not even an Israelite, but the Jebusite king of Salem (which later, after the Israelite conquest, became Jerusalem), and a 'priest of God Most High' (v. 1, NEB), who uses that title rather than the Israelite 'Yahweh' in his formula of blessing (Genesis 14:18–20).

These are some of the raw materials around which our author is now ready to weave his complex argument for Jesus as the ultimate and eternal high priest.

The story in a nutshell

First, he reminds his readers of the original story. After Abraham's famous defeat of four invading kings (in order to rescue his nephew Lot, whom they had captured), as he was returning with the spoils of battle, King Melchizedek came out to meet him with gifts of food and drink and gave him a priestly blessing in the name of 'God Most High'; in return Abraham gave him a tenth of the spoils (just as later the Israelites were to maintain their priests with an offering of a tenth of everything). And that's all there is to it: not a very substantial basis for a theological argument, we might think.

What's in a name?

Then he draws attention to the meaning of the names Melchi-zedek 'king of righteousness' and Salem (the old name of Jerusalem) which he links with Shalom, 'peace'. Nothing will be built specifically on these interpretations, but they serve further to prepare us to explore how Melchizedek may relate to Jesus, the Prince of Peace, and the one through whom God's righteousness has been revealed.

An argument from silence

Perhaps the most striking feature of the figure of Melchizedek in Genesis is the mysterious way in which this clearly important person just appears in the narrative and disappears again with almost nothing to satisfy our curiosity as to who he is. And that is the feature which the author now draws into his argument. As far as the story goes, Melchizedek has no family, no genealogy; he is not born and he does not die. In his very rootlessness and timelessness he thus forms a suitable model for the one who was to come, the Son (not of any man but) of God, who shares God's eternal existence, and can thus uniquely exercise that eternal priesthood which Psalm 110:4 has claimed to be the prerogative of the 'order of Melchizedek' (6:20).

But surely the real man behind the story did have a family, and was born and died. So isn't the author playing a rather pointless game with the words of Genesis 14? Did *he* really believe that the historical Melchizedek was eternal? I doubt whether he considered the question. His argument is from the text, not from history, and in the silence of the Genesis text, together with the 'for ever' of Psalm 110:4, he finds the material he needs for building up a portrait of the new Melchizedek priest, the eternal Son of God.

It is not the way we do exegesis. But it must have satisfied him, and he must have assumed that his readers too would find here food for fruitful thought.

FOR REFLECTION

Is it possible for us to learn from the theology of the New Testament writers even when we find their methods of interpretation unconvincing?

69 HEBREWS 7:4–10

GREATER *than* ABRAHAM

A complex argument

We are familiar by now with our author's arguments for the superiority of Jesus to figures from the Old Testament. He is now developing another such argument, but this one works rather differently. Instead of a straight comparison between Jesus and the Old Testament person (prophets, angels, Moses, Joshua) we now have a three-cornered argument, with Melchizedek coming in as the middle figure. In these verses Jesus is not mentioned at all: it is the superiority of Melchizedek to Abraham that is at issue, though the purpose of establishing this is so that the author can go on to transfer this status to Jesus, as the new Melchizedek.

Moreover, while the immediate comparison is with Abraham, that is not the point he is aiming for. There is, perhaps surprisingly, no argument in Hebrews directly for the superiority of Jesus to Abraham. What this chapter is aiming to establish is rather the superiority of Jesus, the priest 'according to the order of Melchizedek', to the Levitical priests of the Old Testament tabernacle, the sons of Aaron. But in the Old Testament, Melchizedek is not brought into contact with Aaron or his sons, but only with Abraham. So it is by way of Abraham, as the ultimate ancestor of the Levitical priests (as of all Israelites!), that the author must set up his argument.

There are thus now four members in this comparison: Melchizedek the priest is superior to Abraham, and thus also to Abraham's descendants, the Levitical priests; and therefore Jesus, the priest 'according to the order of Melchizedek', also exercises a priesthood superior to theirs. That is where the argument is going, and it is interesting that no attempt is made to establish Jesus as in turn superior to Melchizedek. He belongs to the 'order of Melchizedek', and that is all that is needed.

Tithes and blessing

Two priestly themes emerge from the Melchizedek story. First, the payment of tithes, which, as the author points out in verse 5, are a distinctive prerogative of the Old Testament priests, and which symbolize their special status in relation to the rest of Israel. Yet in Genesis 14 we find this other priest, 'who does not belong to their ancestry' (v. 6), receiving tithes even from the patriarch Abraham himself. And Abraham was the great-grandfather of Levi, the patriarch of the priestly tribe. So the author rather quaintly pictures Levi, the priestly ancestor, himself paying tithes to Melchizedek when he was still 'in the loins of his ancestor' (v. 10). Melchizedek thus stands supreme above all the later priests of the Old Testament.

Then there is the blessing, one of the central functions of the Levitical priests (Numbers 6:22–27). But their ancestor Abraham had himself been blessed by Melchizedek, and 'the inferior is blessed by the superior' (v. 7). Even Abraham, 'who had received the promises' (v. 6) of God's special blessing on him (Genesis 12:1–3), submitted to the blessing offered by this extraordinary priest-king of Salem. This puts Melchizedek on the highest possible level under 'God Most High'.

Exit Melchizedek

With that, Melchizedek has served his purpose in this letter, and will not appear again except in further references to the 'order of Melchizedek' which Psalm 110:4 envisages. If it shares the status of Melchizedek, this 'order' must be on a far higher level than the priesthood of the Old Testament (the 'order of Aaron', v. 11), superior even to the original ancestor of Israel himself, and therefore to all his descendants, whether priestly or not. It is that 'order' which will enable our author to claim for Jesus a single, eternal priesthood far above all earthly priests. There is thus no need to raise the question of the relative importance of Jesus and Melchizedek, since it was not Melchizedek and his 'order' which was the concern of Jewish religion, but rather the 'order of Aaron'. Melchizedek can therefore exit as mysteriously as he came in, and leave his successor-priest Jesus in possession of the stage.

FOR REFLECTION

This is, for us, a pretty remote and abstruse argument. Try to put yourself in the place of a Jew who had been brought up to respect the Levitical priests as God's representatives and to depend on them for spiritual help, and think what they might have made of these verses.

70 HEBREWS 7:11–19

A NEW TYPE *of* PRIESTHOOD

We now turn to a more direct comparison of Jesus' priesthood with that of the Old Testament. The argument is based not now on Melchizedek himself, as he appears in Genesis 14, but rather on the idea of a priestly 'order of Melchizedek' as it is introduced in Psalm 110:4.

The end of the old order

When the psalm speaks of a new order of priesthood, it implies that the old order, the Levitical 'order of Aaron', is no longer valid. It failed to bring 'perfection', the goal towards which, as we have seen, God is leading his people. And associated with the priesthood in this failure is the Old Testament law itself, the law according to which the priests operated and which it was their responsibility to teach and enforce. The law too proved to be 'weak and ineffectual', and unable to make anything perfect (vv. 18–19), and so both priesthood and law were ripe for abolition. It is that 'abrogation' (v. 18) which is implied by the appointment of a new 'priest for ever according to the order of Melchizedek'.

Other New Testament writers are more cautious in dealing with the Old Testament law. Even Paul, who rejoices to be 'free from the law' (Galatians 3:23–26; 4:4–5), still regards the law itself as good, and speaks in terms of its fulfilment rather than its abrogation. Hebrews is more radical, and the author's language here will be matched in the next chapter when he talks about the old covenant as a whole as 'obsolete' (8:13). No doubt this is partly because his readers, as good Jews, still felt a strong loyalty to the Old Testament law, and he wants them to feel free to move on. But he goes further in the direction of completely repudiating the Old Testament law than other Jewish Christians in the first century seem to have been comfortable with.

The focus, however, remains for now on the priesthood, as the new priesthood promised in Psalm 110:4 is further described.

New qualifications for priesthood

The primary qualification for being a priest in the Old Testament was to have been born into the right family, in the tribe of Levi. By that test

Jesus could not be a priest, because he came from the royal family of David (which belonged to the tribe of Judah), and the priesthood was jealously guarded from royal interference. The statement here that Jesus was from the tribe of Judah no doubt derives from his being known as 'son of David' (see especially Matthew 1, and see Study 27), even though Hebrews never actually uses that title for Jesus.

But the new priesthood has a new entry qualification, 'not physical descent, but the power of an indestructible life' (v. 16). It is, according to Psalm 110:4, a priesthood 'for ever', and so only one who lives for ever can fulfil it. In place of a succession of mortal descendants of Levi, we have the one eternal Son of God, who fits the model of Melchizedek who had 'neither beginning of days nor end of life' (7:3). Melchizedek was from no Israelite tribe, but he was a king and a priest. His successor from the royal tribe of Judah likewise brings together in one person the two key Old Testament offices of king and priest, and holds them now for ever.

A better hope

Over against the ineffectiveness of the old law and its priesthood stands now a new and 'better' hope (v. 19). The old system brought only frustration, as the purification obtained by one sacrifice was overtaken by further sin and another sacrifice was needed, and then another. There was no end to it, no *hope* of a more permanent relationship with God. But now through the priestly work of Christ and his one perfect sacrifice, hope is restored, and with it an open way to approach God with confidence instead of fear.

PRAYER

Thank you, Lord, for giving us Jesus as our priest and, through him, giving us a better hope. Help us to live in that hope and to enjoy the access to your presence which he has opened up for us through his sacrifice. Amen.

71 HEBREWS 7:20–25

A Priest For Ever

In these verses the author continues his argument for the superiority of the priesthood of Jesus, as compared with that of the Levitical priests of the Old Testament. He focuses on two further lines of thought, each of which has already been at least hinted at in what has gone before, but is now developed more explicitly.

Appointed with an oath

The importance of God's oath, as a guarantee that what he says may be trusted, has already been mentioned in 6:13–18, but at that point the only oath which was actually cited was the oath with which God promised his blessing to Abraham. But we noted then that the author almost certainly already had another oath in mind, the one which he now quotes directly from Psalm 110:4, this time focusing on the first half of the verse. Jesus' priesthood, guaranteed by such a divine oath, thus rests on the surest possible foundation. No such oath undergirded the office of the Old Testament priests.

This difference thus again indicates that what we have with Jesus is 'better' than what went before. That key word is now coming before us more insistently: a 'better hope' (v. 19), a 'better covenant' (v. 22; 8:6), 'better promises' (8:6). Chapter 8 will explore more fully the theme of a 'new covenant', based on the famous prophecy of Jeremiah 31:31–34. This is legal language. A covenant (agreement) is established between God and his people, but such an agreement also requires a third party, as 'mediator' (8:6) and 'guarantor' or 'surety' (v. 22). Both these offices are fulfilled by Jesus, who comes as the 'go-between' between God and his people, and who stands surety for his people's compliance with the terms of the agreement. Our relationship with God could not be in safer hands.

Unending priesthood

The second theme in this section is developed in verses 23–25. It draws directly on the phrase in Psalm 110:4, 'a priest *for ever*'. There has never been such a priesthood before, for the very good reason that the priests were human beings, and they died. A priesthood 'for ever' demands someone who will not die, and that we now have in the eternal Son of God, who, like Melchizedek, has 'neither beginning of days nor end of life' (7:3), and holds his office by 'the power of an indestructible life' (7:16). Under the Old Testament régime there were necessarily many priests, but now we need only one, and he lives and continues his priestly work for ever.

So whereas before there was always a sense of the temporary about the work of the priests (sacrifices which needed to be repeated and priests who needed to be replaced), now salvation is complete and for ever. The phrase in verse 25 may mean either 'completely' or 'for all time' and I doubt if the author would have felt it necessary to choose between the two! With Jesus as our intermediary, there need be no more hesitation in our approach to God, no fear that the system may no longer work. Jesus is always there, and we need no more.

The priest as intercessor

Here, almost in passing, is a further important role of the priest. As representative of the people, he pleads their cause before God, as for instance Moses did in Exodus 32:11–14, 30–32. During his earthly ministry Jesus prayed for his disciples (Luke 22:32; John 17) and he continues that intercession for ever in heaven. This theme, not often expressed in the New Testament, is a great source of pastoral comfort. In Romans 8 Paul speaks both of the intercession of the Spirit on our behalf when we do not know how to pray for ourselves (Romans 8:26) and also of Jesus himself interceding for us at God's right hand (Romans 8:34), and concludes that with such representation we have nothing to fear. So here we are assured that Jesus' priestly work on our behalf consists not only of what he *has* done for us through his atoning death, but also of his *continuing* intercession for us. And of that work there is, thank God, no end.

PRAYER

Lord Jesus, thank you that we need fear nothing, since you represent us at God's right hand. Help us to enjoy the peace and security which that assurance gives. Amen.

Perfect For Ever

With these verses we come to the resounding conclusion of the argument to establish the status of Jesus as the one perfect high priest, who replaces and renders irrelevant all the priestly establishment of the Old Testament. We have not, however, finished with the theme of priesthood, for the author's purpose in establishing Jesus' priestly credentials was to provide the basis for exploring his *work* as priest, especially the work of sacrifice, and that will be our theme through the next three chapters of the letter. The concept of priesthood will never be very far away.

A portrait of the perfect priest

We saw in 5:1–10 that the priest should be fully identified with the people whom he represents, and that he should be called by God to this task. For ordinary priests, the full identification with the people means a share not only in their human weakness but also in their sinfulness, so that the priest must include his own sins with those of the people for whom he offers sacrifice. Jesus, however, is not like that. He is indeed identified with all our human experience, and he has 'learned obedience through suffering' (5:7–10), but all this 'without sin' (4:15). Here, then, is a new and far more wonderful kind of priest, fully able to sympathize with his people and thus to intercede for them, but morally unstained. Such a priest is 'fitting' (v. 26), and the author goes on to spell out this new quality of priesthood.

The five descriptions in verse 26 all point in the same direction: Jesus is essentially different from us. The author has already established Jesus' solidarity with our condition (2:10–18; 4:15; 5:7–9), and does not need to repeat that argument. But here is the other side of the coin. 'Holy', 'blameless' and 'undefiled' are more or less synonyms—Jesus is negatively without fault, and positively shares the holy character of God. 'Separated from sinners' emphasizes how in this he is distinct, unique, and totally unlike all other (sinful) priests. 'Exalted above the heavens' reminds us where Jesus, as the Son of God, really belongs. After his temporary period of being 'lower than the angels', he has returned to his true home, and it is there, not in an earthly sanctuary, that he now carries out his priestly work on our behalf.

No sins of his own

In verse 27 we return to the issue raised in 5:2–3, the sinfulness of all other priests, and therefore their need to offer sacrifices also for themselves. Jesus, by contrast, is unencumbered by sin of his own; he himself has no need of sacrifice, and so the sacrifice he offers is entirely for others and thus can be fully effective for those he represents.

And whereas previous sacrifices needed to be constantly repeated, because sin constantly recurred, Jesus' sacrifice needs no repetition. Here the author introduces an important expression which we will meet several times in the following discussion of sacrifice, 'once for all' (see 9:12, 26, 28; 10:10, 12). Once Jesus has died on the cross, no further atonement is needed or possible: he has done it all.

The time of fulfilment

The Old Testament priesthood, with its constant succession of priests, derived from the law received by Moses at Sinai. It was some centuries later that Psalm 110 was written, with its vision of a single 'priest for ever' (Psalm 110:4). This vision thus represents a later and more advanced stage in God's ongoing purpose with his people. The temporary and imperfect priesthood must give way to one which is permanent, a new order which fulfils the pattern foreshadowed but inadequately embodied in the old. With the appointment of the Son as a priest for ever according to the order of Melchizedek, the perfect priesthood is established. 'Perfect for ever'!

FOR REFLECTION

Compare the following two quotations from the service of Holy Communion in the Book of Common Prayer:

[Christ] 'made there (by his one oblation of himself once offered) a full, perfect, and sufficient sacrifice, oblation and satisfaction for the sins of the whole world.'

'We are unworthy, through our manifold sins, to offer unto thee any sacrifice.'

What are the implications of this 'once for all' language for understanding the nature of our worship today?

73 HEBREWS 8:1–6

The HEAVENLY SANCTUARY

When the Old Testament priesthood was established, it was in order to offer sacrifices in the tabernacle which Moses first set up in the wilderness, and which later became the centre of worship in the promised land. In the time of Solomon the mobile tabernacle was replaced by a fixed temple in Jerusalem, and it was here, and only here, that the priestly ministry of sacrifice took place.

But now we have a new priest, Jesus the Son of God, so where is his sanctuary?

The true tabernacle

The author has already supplied the answer. Our high priest has 'passed through the heavens' (4:14), and is 'seated at the right hand of the throne of the Majesty in the heavens' (v. 1). His offering was indeed made on earth, in Jerusalem (though not, of course, in the temple because he did not belong to the Levitical priesthood). But the sanctuary in which he now appears on our behalf is, of course, in heaven. It is not a mere human artefact, but the true sanctuary which owes its origin to God himself.

In order to establish the superiority of this heavenly sanctuary, the author draws on the words which God spoke to Moses in Exodus 25:40, instructing him to make the original tabernacle 'according to the pattern that was shown you on the mountain'. The 'pattern' there referred to need be no more than the detailed verbal description of the mobile sanctuary which takes up most of chapters 25—30 of Exodus, and which was delivered to Moses by God on the mountain. But the Greek word for 'pattern' is *typos* (from which we derive our words 'type' and 'typology'), and our author seems to have concluded from this that Moses received not merely a set of instructions, but also a vision of the real thing, the true heavenly original of which his earthly construction was to be a faithful copy. (Some people think that this idea is influenced by the teaching of the Greek philosopher Plato that every earthly reality is an imperfect copy of the perfect 'form' in which that thing exists in heaven; but, at least on the surface, the argument in Hebrews derives not from Plato but from the book of Exodus.)

Here, then, is another argument for the superiority of Christ. The Old Testament priests served in a building which was a mere copy and 'shadow' of the real thing; Christ, who would not in any case have been qualified by birth to serve in that sanctuary, carries out his ministry instead in the true, the heavenly sanctuary. The former sanctuary in Jerusalem has become irrelevant.

Incidentally, it is at this point, as I mentioned in Study 46, that we might have expected some comment on the destruction of the Jerusalem temple, if it had already happened. What better proof could there be that the old sanctuary had passed its sell-by date? The fact that the writer of Hebrews does not play that card seems to me to suggest that he was writing before the temple was in fact destroyed in AD70.

A 'more excellent ministry'

The phrase 'a more excellent ministry' (v. 6) is a stronger variant on the repeated theme of 'better'. What goes on in the heavenly sanctuary is clearly on a different level altogether from what takes place in Jerusalem, just as the high priest of that sanctuary is altogether superior to the priests of the Old Testament worship.

And so our author rubs in the point with two more 'better's. Just as the original tabernacle was set up to maintain the relationship between God and his chosen people, newly bound to him by a solemn covenant at Sinai, so Christ is now the go-between for a 'better covenant', a new type of relationship between God and his people (see comments on 7:22). And the basis of that covenant is 'better promises', not now the promise of an earthly territory in Canaan but of heavenly 'rest'. The nature of those promises, and the faith which looks forward to their fulfilment, will be the theme of chapter 11.

PRAYER

Lord, keep us from being satisfied with shadows. May we rather 'set our minds on the things that are above', knowing that our true life is 'hidden with Christ in God' (Colossians 3:1–4). Amen.

74 HEBREWS 8:7–13

A New Covenant

The repeated reference to a 'better covenant' (7:22; 8:6) leads the author into his next point of comparison between the old order and the new, the change from the old covenant to a new one. The covenant which God established with his people at Sinai was at the heart of Israel's national identity, of their understanding of themselves as God's chosen people. To speak of a *new* covenant is therefore a daring and radical idea. But it is not a new idea!

Jeremiah's prophecy

The Old Testament prophets were well aware that all was not well in the relationship between God and his people. The repeated calls to Israel to 'return' to their God in repentant obedience were an eloquent testimony to her failure to keep her side of the agreement. In the great prophecy of Jeremiah 31:31–34, which is here quoted in full, the idea of a renewal of the covenant reached its fullest expression.

The old covenant has not worked, because of Israel's disobedience. So God proposes not simply to re-establish the same covenant on the same terms, but to set up a completely new type of relationship. It will be based not on laws written on stone and paper, but on a law written on people's hearts—internal, not external. So they will no longer need someone else to guide them in their relationship with God, because 'they shall all know me' (v. 11) for themselves. And this personal knowledge of God on which the new covenant is based will be achieved by God's generous writing off of their past sins. There will be a clean sheet, a new start, with its focus not on people's ability to keep a set of laws, but on God's grace.

It is in this brave vision of the prophet over 600 years ago that our author has found the key to understanding the radical change which has come about with the coming of God's Son. He first sets Jeremiah's prophecy out in full in these verses, with a brief explanatory comment in verse 13. Then he will explore in the next two chapters how this new relationship is established and maintained by Jesus' sacrifice of himself (in contrast to Moses' covenant sacrifices of animals at Sinai, Exodus 24:3–8), before he concludes his argument with a triumphant return to the words of Jeremiah in 10:16–17.

Jeremiah 31:31–34 thus functions as the 'text' which undergirds the whole exposition of the new covenant in these chapters.

Obsolete

The vision of a new covenant implies dissatisfaction with the old (v. 7). But it was not the covenant itself which was at fault, but the people with whom it was made. That is why in verse 8 the author talks about God finding fault not with 'it' but with *them*, the Israelites of the old covenant. It was because they could not meet the terms of the agreement that it has lapsed.

The point is explained more fully in verse 13. By speaking of a new covenant, God has 'made old' (literally) the former one. It thus belongs to the past. And since it (literally) 'is being made old' and 'is ageing', it cannot be expected to continue, but must be about to disappear. I have translated the Greek terms literally so as to make clear that the word 'obsolete', which English translations tend to use here, is perhaps a little too definite and negative. It is a matter of 'ageing', so that the old covenant has come to the end of its useful life and is now ready for an honourable retirement.

Such language should not be misunderstood. There is no thought that the old covenant was a mistake, nor that the Old Testament scriptures which chart its course can be written off as worthless. The whole argument of Hebrews is based on the Old Testament, as the 'living and active word of God' (4:12). It is not that it was wrong, but that it was not God's *last* word. Now, with the coming of the Son, that last word has been spoken, and we are called to move on to better things, leaving behind that phase of God's relationship with his people which, for all its glories, was only a stage on the way to 'perfection'.

PRAYER

Thank you, Lord, for a new covenant, for the possibility of the forgiveness of sins, of your law in our hearts, of knowing you for ourselves. May our experience of you match up to Jeremiah's vision so long ago, as you have brought it to reality through your Son, Jesus Christ. Amen.

75 HEBREWS 9:1–10

LESSONS *from the* OLD SANCTUARY

The old sanctuary, which we thought about in 8:1–6 in contrast with the heavenly sanctuary, still has lessons to teach us. It is curious that our author always talks about the original tabernacle (tent) rather than the solid temple which succeeded it. This was Israel's first national sanctuary, the one which is described in detail in the law of Moses; and it is that ancient description rather than the contemporary worship centre in Jerusalem which the author uses as his base for thinking about the 'better' worship of the heavenly sanctuary.

The paraphernalia of worship

In verses 2–5 the author briefly describes the structure and contents of the tabernacle as they are set out in Exodus 25—30, but excuses himself from offering a detailed explanation. It is intriguing to wonder what he would have said if he *had* felt it appropriate to 'speak in detail' about these things. Would he have gone into the sort of detailed allegorical exploration of the spiritual symbolism in each piece of furniture, in the way the Jewish philosopher Philo of Alexandria would have done—and as many Christian preachers have done up to this day? We cannot know, since he does not tell us. His interest is not in the physical contents of the tabernacle so much as in the ceremonies that were conducted in it.

Priestly duties

The outer section of the sanctuary (called the 'Holy Place' in verse 2) was where the regular rituals took place (although animal sacrifices were offered outside the Holy Place, on the main altar). It was open only to the priests, and every priest was involved in this duty. But once a year, on the Day of Atonement, the high priest alone was allowed to go beyond the second curtain into the 'Holy of Holies', the inner sanctuary where the ark of God was kept. He took with him the blood of a bull and a goat, which he sprinkled on and around the ark to make atonement for his own sins and for the sins of the people (see Leviticus 16 for the full ceremonial). But no one else was ever allowed inside the Holy of Holies. It is this fact that the author focuses on in his comment in verse 8: the way was not yet open;

people were excluded from the presence of God. That was the nature of Israelite worship as long as the old (earthly) sanctuary was in use. From verse 11 onwards the author will explain how things have changed with the coming of Jesus as our new high priest.

Looking forward to a new system

The concluding comments in verses 9–10 draw a wider conclusion. All the worship of the tabernacle was only a temporary provision 'until the time comes to set things right'. The sacrificial system could never really set a person free from sin ('perfect their conscience'), and the many regulations of the Old Testament ritual law dealt merely with external matters of food and drink and bodily cleanness, rather than with spiritual need. All this served only as a pointer to a future time when a sacrifice would be provided which really could change a person's relationship with God, when people could move on from following an external code to knowing God for themselves, as Jeremiah had predicted. And this, the author will go on to show, is what Christ has now brought.

The very negative assessment of Old Testament religion is thus in deliberate contrast with what is to take its place. The phrase which introduces this line of thought in verse 9—'a symbol of the present time'—probably refers specifically to the fact described in verse 8 that a curtain kept people out of the Holy of Holies. That situation symbolizes the separation between God and his people, the sense of exclusion from the divine presence, which was inherent in the whole Old Testament religion. But that was not the way God intended it to be, and so a time must come when matters are 'set right'. The author has thus set up the background for his discussion of the significance of Christ's high priestly work and sacrifice. *This* is the 'better' way of access to God, the time of setting things right.

FOR REFLECTION

How far is it true in your Christian experience that the sense of exclusion has been taken away? Does this argument mean that no 'ritual' is now needed or appropriate?

76 HEBREWS 9:11–14

WORSHIPPING *the* LIVING GOD

From the inadequacy of the old religious system we turn with relief to 'the good things that have come' (v. 11) with the coming of Christ.

The new high priest

Verses 11–12 work out the comparison between the Levitical high priest's role on the Day of Atonement and the atoning work of Christ. First, the sanctuary into which Christ has gone is not the earthly sanctuary of the old tabernacle, but, as we have already seen in 8:1–5, a 'greater and more perfect tent' which is not constructed by human efforts, but exists eternally in heaven. It is surprising that the author speaks of Christ entering the 'Holy Place' rather than the 'Holy of Holies' of the heavenly sanctuary; the phrase is the same as in verse 2, but it is used here in the less technical sense of the 'sanctuary' as a whole (as also in v. 25).

Secondly, the atoning sacrifice is not now 'the blood of goats and calves', but Christ's own blood, offered on the cross. Even though the animal sacrifices of the Old Testament were God's prescribed means for restoring a penitent sinner, they remained only symbolic, and such blood could never actually take away sin (10:4). The self-offering of Jesus is on a quite different level, as we shall hear more fully throughout these two chapters.

Thirdly, Jesus' offering is 'once for all', as we have already seen in 7:27, and therefore his entry into the sanctuary need no longer be a ritual repeated annually, but has taken place 'once for all'. He is no occasional visitor to the presence of God, but is seated permanently at God's right hand. And that means that instead of a temporary alleviation of the problem of sin, he has achieved 'eternal redemption'. His work can never be repeated, and there is no more to be done.

How much more

Verses 13–14 draw out the point of the comparison more fully. The old animal sacrifices (including the ceremony of the red heifer, a ritual for restoring 'cleanness' after defilement, described in detail in Numbers 19) may have had a limited value in restoring a person who had contracted ritual defilement back into a state of ceremonial purity. But this remains at a very superficial level: it changes nothing in terms of the person's essential relationship with a holy God.

But the blood of Christ really does change things. He is himself without sin ('without blemish' echoes again the language of animal sacrifice, which demanded a perfect specimen), and his offering of himself (not a reluctant animal killed against its will) takes place within the divine purpose. Here is one of those places where the New Testament writers, apparently almost by accident, mention all three persons of the Trinity together in a single formula. But it is not by accident, because the divine plan which reached its climax on the cross was a trinitarian act, with God, Christ and the Spirit united in providing by this means the perfect solution to the problem of human sin.

The result is not at the level of merely 'purifying flesh'; it goes much deeper than that, and purifies our conscience, taking away the guilt which keeps sinners away from a holy God. It was just at this level that the old sacrifices proved ineffective (9:9; 10:2). So now we can leave behind the 'dead works' of repeated and ineffective rituals (which should have been left behind as a result of our Christian conversion, 6:1), and enter into a worship appropriate to 'the living God', a dynamic phrase which we have already met in 3:12, and which takes us away from external ceremonies to a personal encounter with a God who is real and active.

This section, and much of what follows, breathes an atmosphere of ancient ritual and animal sacrifice which is quite foreign to most modern readers. To understand the argument, we need to appreciate what it must have been like to try to serve God under that Old Testament system, but also to realize that our author is using this imagery, which was second nature to his Jewish readers, in order to establish an understanding of Christ's redeeming work which leaves it all behind. The challenge for us in our day is to find appropriate ways to explain Christ's saving work which are more accessible to the culture we live in.

PRAYER

Lord, keep us from all 'dead works', and may we grow to understand more fully what it means to worship the 'living God'. Amen.

77 HEBREWS 9:15–22

Why Christ Died

Hebrews continues to explore the imagery of animal sacrifice and how the death of Christ may be understood in the light of it. In these verses the focus becomes even more alien to many modern readers, as the author takes us further into the religious meaning of blood and death.

Two ideas are interwoven here, linked by a word-play on the Greek word *diatheke* which means both 'covenant' and 'will'. It may help with our understanding of the passage if we deal with the two meanings in turn, reversing the order in which Hebrews introduces them.

A new sacrifice for a new covenant

When God entered into a covenant with his people at Sinai, the agreement was marked by a sacrifice, and the blood of that sacrifice played a prominent role in the ceremony, which is recorded in Exodus 24:3–8 (v. 20 quotes Exodus 24:8). In recalling this incident in verses 18–20, our author includes some elements of sacrificial ritual which are not mentioned in the Exodus passage, but which we find elsewhere in the descriptions of Old Testament sacrifices, particularly the ritual of the red heifer in Numbers 19 which we have already seen alluded to in Hebrews 9:13. He goes on in verse 21 to mention further ritual uses of blood, probably thinking mainly of the sprinkling of blood on the Day of Atonement (Leviticus 16:14–19). The whole principle is summed up in the slightly exaggerated observation that 'almost everything' (v. 22) is purified by blood. Certainly, it would be hard to exaggerate the centrality of sacrificial blood in the ritual law of the Old Testament. A new covenant, therefore, demands a new and better sacrifice.

Why all this blood? Because 'the shedding of blood' is the means to the forgiveness of sins, and thus to restoring the people's relationship with God. The principle of atonement in the law is that the animal represents and takes the place of the person offering it, so that its death is accepted in place of the death which that person's sins have earned. And the blood is the visible symbol of life poured out (Leviticus 17:11). So 'without the shedding of blood there is no forgiveness'.

A will requires a death

By describing God's purpose for his people as their 'eternal inheritance' (v. 15), the author steers us into the other meaning of the word *diatheke*, which he has used hitherto in its more normal meaning of 'covenant'. It also means a 'will', which is of course the basis of an 'inheritance'. So God's covenant with his people is also his bequest. But a bequest remains nothing but a piece of paper until the testator dies. It is only through death that the testator's purpose is eventually achieved. Here, then, is another image pointing to the necessity of death.

The imagery is not the same, of course. The death of the sacrificial animal and the death of the testator are quite different concepts, but the coincidence of the two meanings of the same Greek word allows the author to bring them together into a creative new pairing: Christ is *both* the testator through whose death his *diatheke* is made effective, *and also* the sacrificial victim through whose death God's new *diatheke* with his people is ratified.

Without blood, no forgiveness

Here, then, is an ingenious attempt to make sense, within the framework of Old Testament ritual imagery, of the puzzle which has been at the heart of Christian theological debate ever since: why did Jesus have to die? What possible connection can there be between his death long ago and my sin today? All that complex sacrificial ritual, the author is telling us, was a pointer to a truth which one day must be fulfilled in the ultimate sacrifice of the Son of God—the truth that sin is not lightly to be set aside, that atonement is needed, and that we cannot atone for ourselves. The supreme sacrifice of the Son of God on our behalf has solved the problem.

FOR PRAYER

Lord, help us, as the people of the new covenant, never to lose a sense of the supreme importance of what your Son has done for us through his sacrificial death, and even when we do not fully understand, to 'trust in his redeeming blood'. Amen.

ONCE FOR ALL

In these verses we hear again essentially the same arguments for the superiority of Christ's sacrifice, but with some additional angles introduced.

Heaven and earth

Verses 23–24 return to the contrast between an earthly and a heavenly sanctuary. The old tabernacle was only a 'sketch', a copy of the real thing which is in heaven, yet even that inferior copy needed careful purification by sacrifice. How much more, then, does the heavenly sanctuary require 'better sacrifices', and this is what Christ has offered. That is why he has been able to go not into an earthly sanctuary, but into heaven itself, and that is where he now is, appearing before God on our behalf. Here we meet again the idea of Christ's eternal intercession for his people which was briefly introduced in 7:25.

Only one sacrifice

In verses 25–26, Jesus' one sacrifice is again contrasted with the earthly high priest's need to make atonement each year. If the heavenly sanctuary, of which Christ is the one eternal high priest, had needed such an annual purification, then Christ himself would have had to die repeatedly. But his one sacrifice of himself is sufficient to remove sin for all time, for the past as well as the future.

This decisive, single sacrifice of Christ has been offered 'at the end of the age'. We saw at the very beginning of this letter the conviction that the coming of Christ marked the 'last days' (1:2), and the basic concept of fulfilment which has undergirded the whole argument makes it clear that this is not just another phase in the world's history, but God's last word, his final summing up in Christ of all that has gone before. The New Testament writers often speak in this vein. That sense of climax may seem premature to us as we read their writings two thousand years later. We must recognize that the 'last days' have stretched out much further than any Christian in the first century would have expected. But however long it may take, in principle all has already been achieved. As one commentator has put it, the last chapter was written with the coming of Christ, and since then we have been living in the epilogue.

Looking forward

Verses 27–28 reflect further on this question of finality. Our human life leads up inevitably to death, a once-for-all experience which allows no repetition. After that, all that remains is 'the judgment'—and of course, though the author does not mention it at this point, the outcome of that judgment is either eternal 'rest' (ch. 4) or the loss of it. So also Christ, who has once died for our sins, cannot die again. That is why the story of our redemption is already in principle completed. When he does appear again, it will not be to repeat what he has already done, but to reap the harvest of it by 'saving those who are eagerly waiting for him'. Their salvation has been achieved by the cross; it remains only to be given effect in their experience.

This is a rare reference in Hebrews to the pervasive New Testament theme of Christ's 'second coming'. The author's argument is mainly concerned with what Christ has already done, and its once-for-all efficacy. But he speaks much also of the Christian hope, of the promises of God to his people, and of the faith which endures in the expectation of a heavenly reward. All this is the outcome of what Jesus has done for us, and it is he himself who will one day return to take his people home. It is in the confident expectation of that second coming, and not with any idea that the work of salvation is as yet incomplete, that we look forward to his return to bring the 'last days' to their triumphant conclusion.

PRAYER

Lord Jesus, teach us so to rejoice in your finished work in the past on the cross that we may with sure confidence look forward to your future return. Amen.

79 HEBREWS 10:1–10

'I HAVE COME *to* DO YOUR WILL'

The weary round of animal sacrifices

Verses 1–4 sound what are by now familiar notes, as they explain the inadequacy of the sacrifices offered under the old covenant. The focus falls again on the repetitive nature of the sacrificial system—the same sacrifices offered again and again, but never able to set a person free from the guilt of sin. The very fact that they need to be repeated shows that they have not solved the problem. They serve only to remind one of the reality of sin, not to offer an escape from it.

That is why all that the law prescribed was only a 'shadow of the good things to come'. Compare the language about the Old Testament tabernacle as a 'copy' of the heavenly one (8:5; 9:11, 24). The sacrifices pointed forward to a better and effective sacrifice in the future, and so they whetted the spiritual appetite without ever satisfying it. The 'blood of bulls and goats' served, of course, to restore a person to ritual cleanness for the time being, so that they could properly worship God; but the fundamental need was not for such a temporary lightening of the load, but to 'take away sins', and that they could not do.

Christ's one sacrifice

In Psalm 40:6–8 our author finds the perfect description of what Jesus has come to do.

The quotation begins with a remarkably far-sighted assertion that it is not the sacrifices that really matter to God, but the attitude with which we come to him, an attitude of obedience and commitment to do God's will. The psalmist was thinking of the attitude required of any true worshipper, but our author notices how appropriate the words are to the unique obedience of Christ, and so interprets it more specifically as a poetic description of what happened 'when Christ came into the world'.

He quotes the psalm, as he usually does, from the Greek Septuagint version, and in this case that version is particularly apt: instead of speaking of an 'open ear' (which signifies obedience), the Greek version speaks of God preparing a 'body' (v. 5). The theme of obedience is developed in verse 7 (quoting verse 8 of the psalm), and our author will apply this to Christ's obedience in verse 9. But the specific form which his obedience took was the offering of his 'body' as the one perfect sacrifice, and so this aspect of the Greek wording of the psalm is picked up as well in verse 10. The two themes of obedience and the body are thus woven together into a single powerful statement of the work of Christ on our behalf—another example of the 'creative exegesis' which seems to have come so naturally to the author of Hebrews!

Leaving animal sacrifices behind

Our author's Christ-centred interpretation of Psalm 40:6–8 has thus set in contrast two different approaches to the worship of God. On the one hand there is the whole complex system of animal sacrifice, which the psalm quite clearly regards as failing to offer God the worship he really requires. On the other hand there is the doing of God's will, which is what he really wants to see, and more specifically the doing of God's will by Christ in his offering of his body. These two approaches are explicitly set against one another in verses 8–9, as 'the first' and 'the second'. And when 'the second' has been achieved, 'the first' has no further place; it is 'abolished'.

So for us who live after the coming of Christ, the old system of sacrifice is finished. It never really worked anyway, and now it has been swept aside by something far better. Our purification as the people of God is achieved not by 'the blood of bulls and goats', but by 'the offering of the body of Jesus Christ once for all', because it is in that unique offering that the will of God is truly and finally carried out.

That is what he meant in verse 1 by 'the good things to come'. So it is time to leave the shadows, and to fasten on to the reality.

FOR REFLECTION

Think about the contrast set out in Psalm 40:6–8. Is it true that even since the coming of Christ, there is always a danger of falling back into a reliance on external rituals, and so getting our worship out of perspective?

HEBREWS 10:11–18

A Single Sacrifice *for* Sins

In these verses we come to the climax of the argument which the author has been developing throughout chapters 8—10, to show how in Christ we have at last a full and complete way of salvation. The old system of animal sacrifices, and the old covenant on which it was founded, have failed to provide an effective way of 'taking away sins'. So now they have finally been replaced by the one perfect sacrifice which achieves in reality what they could only hint at.

One sacrifice for ever

'A full, perfect and sufficient sacrifice, oblation and satisfaction for the sins of the whole world.' Those words from the service of Holy Communion in the Anglican *Book of Common Prayer* powerfully summarize the teaching of verses 11–14.

Under the old covenant, there was an unending round of sacrifices, repeated again and again because they were never able to offer a permanent solution to the problem of human sinfulness. The very repetitiousness of the priests' service demonstrated its ultimate ineffectiveness. But now, over against this frustrating round of sacrifices stands the one perfect sacrifice offered by the great high priest himself. It is a single sacrifice, and it is effective for all time.

Once that sacrifice has been offered, there is no more for Christ to do to win our salvation. To illustrate the point, our author returns yet again to Psalm 110, and points out that verse 1 speaks of the 'Lord' now *sitting* at God's right hand, his work completed.

It is that sense of completion which lies behind what verse 14 says about 'perfecting' those who are sanctified. Several times our author has talked about 'perfection', not primarily in the sense of moral flawlessness, but of a task fully performed. When he spoke in 2:10 and 5:9 of Jesus being 'made perfect', he was thinking of his being now fully equipped to carry out his saving mission, and now that that mission has been accomplished, he can speak again of 'perfection'. A 'perfect salvation' has been achieved. That is the point of 'perfection' language here, and it would be quite inappropriate to take verse 14 out of context to be used as ammunition in the theological argument over whether it is possible for a Christian to attain (moral) 'perfection' in this life. Christ's one sacrifice has provided all that is needed for our 'sanctification'—but it is not the aim of these verses to pronounce on how far that sanctification may or may not be completed during our earthly pilgrimage.

Indeed, in his use of Psalm 110:1 here our author draws our attention to the paradox of a salvation which is complete and yet not finished. The Christ who sits in triumphant authority at God's right hand is none the less still 'waiting' (v. 13). His enemies are yet to be totally subdued 'beneath his footstool'. The war has been won, but there is a mopping-up operation still to be carried out. The author of Hebrews was conscious of living, as we still live, in the interim, still looking forward to the day when 'at the name of Jesus every knee shall bow' (Philippians 2:10).

Back to Jeremiah's prophecy

The great vision of Jeremiah which was quoted in full in 8:8–12 is now brought back into the argument to round off this section of the letter. This time our author quotes only the key phrases which sum up the basis of the new covenant, a relationship with God based not on external rules and regulations but on his people knowing God and his will for themselves, and also (v. 17) on their sins being forgiven and forgotten. It is that thrilling prospect which has been brought into reality by Christ's one perfect sacrifice. As a result, sin can be truly and freely forgiven and forgotten, and when that has happened, no more sacrifice is needed. The old treadmill is broken; sin has been 'taken away'; the way into the very presence of God is thrown open to all who share in the benefit of Christ's sacrifice.

With that, the theological argument is complete. It remains for the author now only to draw out its implications for his readers, and to urge them to take full advantage of the great salvation which God has provided for them through his Son.

PRAYER

Thank you, Lord Jesus, for providing the way for us to be free of our sins. Help us so to receive that forgiveness that your great sacrifice may not have been in vain. Amen.

81 HEBREWS 10:19–25

MAKING *the* MOST *of* IT

The 'better' way of salvation through Jesus has been explained at length. But the author's aim has not been merely to establish its theoretical superiority to the way of the old covenant, but to encourage his readers to discover and enjoy its richness in experience as well. It is not enough just to understand the perfect saving work of Christ: they must enter into it for themselves.

Privileged access

The imagery of the Day of Atonement is still in the author's mind. Only one person was allowed to enter the Holy of Holies, and that only once a year, carrying the blood of an animal sacrifice. Everyone else was excluded by the curtain, and by the sinfulness which made them unworthy to enter the presence of God. But now Jesus, our high priest, has gone in—not into the earthly sanctuary, but into the heavenly; not with animal blood, but with his own (9:11–12). That one perfect sacrifice has opened the way not only for him but for all who come with him, relying on his sacrificial blood.

So the curtain is now open. Thinking no doubt of the Gospel account of the curtain of the temple being torn at the moment of Jesus' death (Mark 15:38), in verse 20 the author links that tearing with the tearing of Jesus' flesh on the cross. So it is through his death that the way has been opened, a new way, and a 'living' way which dispenses once and for all with the 'dead works' of animal sacrifice (9:14).

Confidence

So now, instead of the fear and trembling of the old ritual, we can come to God in full confidence, invited and introduced by none other than the great high priest himself, Jesus the Son of God. Verses 22 and 23 exude confidence: 'a true heart', 'full assurance of faith', hearts set free from bad conscience, 'holding fast the confession of our hope'. This letter is written to people who are uncertain, diffident, fearful, 'wavering'. But if only they will understand the nature of the salvation Christ has won, there is no need for fear, for their access to the presence of God depends not on their own worthiness, but on the faithfulness of the one who has promised them salvation.

In verse 22 the basis of the Christian disciple's confidence is expressed in the double form of 'hearts sprinkled clean' and 'bodies washed with pure water'. The mention of 'washed bodies' may seem surprising, when the whole thrust of the argument seems to be away from external ritual towards spiritual reality. But Christianity has not dispensed with the physical, and baptism in water is, as the old Catechism put it, the 'outward and visible sign' of spiritual cleansing. As such, it is a valuable support for our confidence in approaching God; it is the symbol of our new life in Christ. That is why both John the Baptist and Jesus spoke of the need for baptism in both water and Spirit (Mark 1:8; John 1:33; 3:5).

Encouraging one another

So there is every reason for confidence. But human nature is weak, and we need the support of other disciples to keep us up to the mark. Verses 24–25 sound a pastorally important note—the mutual responsibility of God's people to encourage and challenge one another to live up to our high calling. Apparently the author has heard that some of the group, demoralized by persecution and by their own doubts, have given up attending the church's gatherings. That way lies defeat. A solitary disciple, lacking the stimulus of Christian fellowship, is a vulnerable disciple. Moreover, it is not the absentee only who suffers, but the fellowship is weakened by the lack of the 'provocation' to love and good works which their presence ought to provide for all the others. There is a sense of urgency about this appeal, not only because of their imminent danger of 'drifting' and losing their faith, but also because the time may be short. As so often in the New Testament, the expectation of the Lord's coming provides not an invitation to speculation but a spur to responsible Christian living.

FOR REFLECTION

Is the Church today equally in danger of losing its sense of privilege and of confident hope? How far do the exhortations of these verses need to be taken to heart in the church to which you belong?

82 HEBREWS 10:26–31

Another SOLEMN WARNING

In 6:4–8 we have already heard words like these, an uncompromising warning of the danger of turning back. Here again we face the uncomfortable question of whether it is possible for a true Christian to lose their salvation altogether. Here again we are confronted with the possibility of a final apostasy from which there is no turning back. It would be a good idea at this point to look back at the notes on that passage (Study 65), and the questions which I raised there about the right way to understand these fierce warnings in the light of assurances elsewhere in the New Testament that God's people cannot be snatched from his hand.

Note that following this passage the author will again make it clear in verses 32–39, as he did in 6:9–12, that he does not regard his readers as having reached the point of no return. He is concerned, but has not despaired of them. But it is time for another shot across the bows.

The other side of the coin

After the warm confidence of 10:19–23, these verses come as an unwelcome dash of cold water. But if there is now a 'new and living way' for us to follow, then there are bound to be serious consequences if it is *not* followed. And the mention of people who are dropping out of Christian fellowship (10:24–25) brings forward the chilling prospect of what might happen to them if they persist in this course.

The author is speaking of *deliberately* renouncing a previously held faith. He speaks of people who have 'received the knowledge of the truth' but then 'wilfully persist in sin' (v. 26), and of those who 'profane the blood of the covenant by which they were sanctified' (v. 29). These are apparently people who have not just heard about salvation through Christ, but have experienced it for themselves, so that when they turn away they are 'spurning the Son of God' and 'outraging the Spirit of grace', just as he spoke in 6:6 about 'crucifying again the Son of God and holding him up to contempt'. All this indicates wilful apostasy rather than merely 'drifting'. But his concern is that spiritual carelessness may lead to this more open rebellion if his readers are not careful to support and encourage one another.

The vengeance of God

We do not talk so much these days, as these verses do so powerfully, about God as judge and avenger. But this sterner side of God's nature is no less central in the Bible. The same 'living God' whom we delight to worship (9:14) is not to be trifled with (v. 31). He is not only a loving Father but also 'a consuming fire' (12:29). Some people imagine that with the coming of Christ we can forget about all the harsh language of punishment in the Old Testament, but Jesus also spoke about hell and judgment, and verses 28–29 remind us that because the salvation on offer is now on a higher level, so also the stakes are higher for those who decide to reject God's offer.

When our author speaks of 'outraging the Spirit of grace' we are reminded of Jesus' solemn words about the irrevocable consequences of 'blasphemy against the Holy Spirit' (Mark 3:28–29). Such a blatant and total rejection of the light that has once been received cannot be condoned. It is possible to go too far in challenging God.

The logic of this argument is perhaps summed up best in verse 26: 'There no longer remains a sacrifice for sins'. If Christ's sacrifice is 'once and for all', and has made other sacrifices obsolete, then when a person has once been saved through that sacrifice, and then rejects it, there is no other to be had. If salvation is once for all, then so also must be the deliberate rejection of that salvation. It is indeed a 'fearful prospect' (v. 27).

FOR REFLECTION

It is sometimes suggested that the God of the Old Testament is a God of vengeance whereas the God of the New Testament is a God of love. What do you think?

83 HEBREWS 10:32–39

LIVING *by* FAITH

After the stick, the carrot! (See Study 66 for the same pastoral method.) The fierce warning of 10:26–31 was intended to pull the readers up short, and to force them to think seriously about the consequences of turning back from their Christian commitment. But of course the author has 'dangled them over hell' in order to save them from it, and now the warmth of pastoral encouragement takes the place of the rhetoric of judgment.

You have come so far already

In verses 32–34 he reminds them of the Christian pilgrimage they have already undertaken since they first 'saw the light'. It has not been an easy road. The warnings Jesus gave to his first disciples about the unpopularity and suffering which would come to those who identified with him (Matthew 10:16–39; John 15:18–25 and so on) proved true for later believers as well. For this particular group the focus has no doubt been on the ostracism and persecution which came from their fellow Jews who did not recognize Jesus as the Messiah, just as we find throughout the narratives in the book of Acts. A Christian Jew in the first century was in a very exposed position, and they have not been shielded from the onslaught.

But they have discovered in their shared sufferings, as persecuted Christians have so often found since, the rich experience of Christian solidarity. They have discovered what it means to belong to the body of Christ in which 'if one member suffers, all suffer together' (1 Corinthians 12:26). And so they have borne it all 'cheerfully', not just with grim determination, but with a shrewd awareness that they have the best of the bargain! What they have lost through following Christ bears no comparison with what they have gained, 'something better and more lasting'.

After all that, what folly it would be to throw it all away (v. 35).

Faith and 'shrinking back'

To reinforce this point, the author now introduces another of his key texts from the Old Testament, one which was also a favourite of the apostle Paul, Habakkuk 2:3–4. The words Paul loved to quote were 'the righteous will live by faith' (Romans 1:17; Galatians 3:11): they became the basic text for Paul's explanation of 'justification by faith' as the essence of Christian salvation, underlying much of the argument of Romans 1—8. Hebrews, however, quotes the text more fully, and so sets Paul's favourite slogan more clearly in its context. Habakkuk contrasts the proud, whose 'spirit is not right in them', with the 'righteous' who in faith wait patiently for the fulfilment of God's promised salvation. It is these 'righteous' who are the model our author wants his readers to follow by sticking it out until God's promises are fulfilled. He thus uses this text with closer attention to its original sense than Paul does (see Study 48).

The text is not quite as in our Old Testament. Hebrews quotes the Greek Septuagint version, which does not speak of 'the proud' but of one who 'shrinks back' (v. 38). The author also reverses the order of the two clauses in Habakkuk 2:4 so that the attitude of 'faith' comes before its converse, 'shrinking back'.

It is these two attitudes which then form the basis of the author's appeal. You have begun in faith, and must not now 'shrink back'. You have shown great endurance already: just keep it up a bit longer. God's promises are sure, even though they have not yet materialized. But this has always been the mark of the true people of God—to go on trusting God through the dark times, knowing that his light will dawn. It is those who hold on in faith who will receive what God has promised, but to give it up now is to be lost. And, says the author with a pastorally sensitive use of the first person in verse 39, *we* belong to the people of faith, not to the 'shrinkers'.

So the scene is set for the great celebration of faith which will run right through chapter 11, reaching its magnificent climax in 12:1–2. The whole passage is a sort of extended exposition of Habakkuk 2:3–4. Hebrews 11:1 does not introduce a new subject, but develops the meaning of the persevering 'faith' for which 10:35–39 has called.

PRAYER

You know, Lord, the temptation to shrink back when things get difficult for us as Christians. Help us to keep a clear sense of priorities, to take firm hold of your promises, and so to persevere as your faith-ful people. Amen.

84 HEBREWS 11:1–6

SEEING *the* INVISIBLE

What is 'faith'?

'Faith' means many different things to different people. But the author here spells out clearly in verse 1 how he is using it in this chapter. 'The assurance of things hoped for' points to a firm grasp on God's promises, even though they remain still in the future, while 'the conviction of things not seen' speaks of those who can see beyond their immediate circumstances to more ultimate reality, and especially to the reality of the unseen God. Note how these two ideas are expressed again in verse 6—God's existence, and his rewards.

These twin perspectives might be summarized as 'looking forward' and 'looking up'. Both aspects will be illustrated again and again in this chapter from the lives of Old Testament characters, to whom God and his promises were more real than the often threatening circumstances in which they lived. They pressed on in faith, refusing to be cowed by persecution or discouraged by present hardship, because they 'considered him faithful who had promised' (v. 11).

It is this attitude of faith which Habakkuk 2:3–4 has called for (10:36–39) and which the readers of the letter need in their present state of doubt and fear. It remains for us today the secret of effective discipleship in a hostile or sceptical world.

Faith in the creator God

The account of 'faith' in the Old Testament starts at the beginning, with Genesis 1 and 2. This is not, as in the rest of the chapter, an example of faith exercised by people long ago, but of faith as *our* basis for understanding the story of creation. In contrast to those who can see only the 'visible' things of the material universe, faith grasps the reality behind them. To the eyes of faith, the created world is itself a testimony to the 'things not seen', to the God who made it. After all the philosophical arguments have been rehearsed and refined, it remains in the end a matter of faith. There will always be those who cannot see beyond the surface level, and argument alone will not persuade them. This is the realm of faith.

The first two witnesses

In 12:1, looking back over this chapter, the author will speak of a 'cloud of witnesses' drawn from the stories of the Old Testament who encourage us, like them, to live the life of faith. The list begins in the very early chapters of Genesis, with Abel (Genesis 4:1–9) and Enoch (Genesis 5:21–24).

The Genesis story does not say what it was about Abel's animal sacrifice which proved more acceptable to God than his brother's cereal offering (though there is perhaps a hint in Genesis 4:7), but our author traces the difference to Abel's faith (v. 4), which contrasts with Cain's violent resentment. No doubt one reason for choosing this example was that Abel, as the first victim of murder, formed a suitable model for those who were facing the possibility of martyrdom at the hands of their faithless 'brothers'. Even in his death, Abel still speaks (compare Genesis 4:10): it is he, rather than his apparently triumphant brother, who is remembered as a man of God.

Enoch's story is even slighter (v. 5), but what has attracted our author's attention is the repeated assertion that he 'walked with God'. This is taken (following the Septuagint translation) to mean that he 'pleased God', that there was a relationship of trust and fellowship between Enoch and his God which transcended the limits of this earthly life. So the mysterious words, 'He was not, because God took him' were taken to mean that Enoch had no need to pass through death, and so he and Elijah (and, in a rather different way, Moses) were celebrated in Jewish tradition as the 'deathless ones'.

Such a relationship, which links earth and heaven in a single continuum, is of the essence of faith. Even the rest of us, who, unlike Enoch, will die, need not fear that death if we have the faith which pleases God.

FOR REFLECTION

Compare Paul's words about 'hope' in Romans 8:18–25. Is there any difference between that idea and what Hebrews means by 'faith'?

85 HEBREWS 11:7–12

NOAH & ABRAHAM

We continue our run through the heroes of faith in the Old Testament with two more characters from the early chapters of Genesis, this time with men who had a central role to play in the development of God's relationship with his human creation, and about whom there are lengthy stories told.

Noah

Noah is introduced in Genesis 6:8–9 as one who 'found favour in the sight of the Lord', and as 'righteous' and 'blameless in his generation'. His character is summed up in the same words which were used for Enoch: he 'walked with God' (Genesis 6:9). It was because of this relationship that he, unlike other people at the time, was warned by God that the flood was coming, and his 'faith' is shown by the fact that he took God at his word, and acted on it. He acted in the light of what was 'as yet unseen'.

Later tradition has made much of the way other people would have mocked Noah's crazy idea of building a huge boat on dry land, and scornfully rejected his attempts to bring them on board. But his obedience to God's warning served to 'condemn' their refusal to take God seriously, and made him a classic example of 'the righteousness that is in accordance with faith' (v. 7). This is close to the classical language of Paul in Romans and Galatians, and while Paul does not develop the comparison, he would probably have been happy to recognize in Noah, as in Abraham, an example of one who believed God, and so found salvation. There is no great distance, then, between the 'justifying faith' of Paul and the 'persevering faith' of Hebrews.

Abraham

As the ancestor of the Hebrew race, Abraham naturally features strongly in this survey of the heroes of faith. We shall hear more about him in the following studies. He comes before us as a conspicuous example of one who believed God's promises against all the odds, and whose faith was abundantly rewarded. In these verses we note two aspects of God's promises to Abraham—the promises of land and of a family.

The promised land

Abraham came from a settled home in Mesopotamia, but God called him to leave, and promised him a new home. So he became a nomad, not knowing even where his new home was to be—another example of taking hold by faith of what is 'as yet unseen'. Eventually his wanderings brought him to the land of Canaan, and God's promise became more specific: *this* was to be his land. But it was not yet his, and though he lived there for many years, it was as a tolerated alien, not as a land-owner. In that sense he never did receive what had been promised. But because the promise was to him and to his descendants, he could look forward to what was yet to be fulfilled, even if not in his own lifetime.

So the author draws a suggestive contrast between the 'tents' of his nomadic life and the future 'city that has foundations' (v. 10). That contrast is a model of the life of faith, able to look beyond the uncertainties and frustrations of the present to the solid reality of a promised future 'whose architect and builder is God'.

The promised son

The fulfilment of God's promise was for Abraham's descendants, but so far he didn't have any, and he and his wife were getting old. The promise of a son and heir to the aged Abraham and Sarah is a key feature in the Genesis stories (Genesis 15:1–6; 17:1–22; 18:9–15). They respond to the promise with a mixture of faith (Genesis 15:6) and incredulity, especially on the part of Sarah (Genesis 17:17; 18:12–15), but faith triumphs in the end. (The more likely reading of the Greek text of verse 11 makes Sarah herself the subject of the verbs 'received power' and 'considered him faithful', though the Genesis story does not suggest this.) Faith thus includes being prepared to trust God even to do that which seems impossible.

PRAYER

Lord, help us to learn from Abraham not to limit your power to what we can get our minds round, and to be willing, like him, to go out on a limb when you call us. Amen.

Seeking *a* Homeland

In the next section we shall return to Abraham, and God's promise to him of a son, but first the roll-call of the heroes of faith pauses for a brief summary of what living by faith meant for the Hebrew patriarchs. In the previous paragraph we have been introduced to Abraham with his wife Sarah, and to their son Isaac and his son Jacob. These, the great founding fathers to whom Israel looked back with such pride, were a model of faith for all those who would follow after them, for all of them remained 'strangers and foreigners on the earth' (v. 13).

The nomadic life

It is clear from the Genesis stories that Abraham began the process of acquiring land in Canaan (Genesis 23) and that Isaac and Jacob were able to settle down to the extent of growing crops, and becoming known and respected residents in the region. They were not constantly on the move with their livestock in true nomadic style. But all the time there was a sense of impermanence. They were newcomers, and their tenure was not secure, until eventually famine forced the family out to Egypt. The contrast between Lot, who went down to settle in the cities of the plain, and Abraham, who stayed in his tent up on the hills (Genesis 13), remained a powerful image for the character of patriarchal life. However successful, they remained 'strangers and foreigners'.

Yet they had God's promise of the land which they were one day to possess as their own. So they lived out their long lives still looking forward to something better which was in store for them, or at least for their descendants. They could have returned to Abraham's former home in Mesopotamia if they wished, but they preferred to hold on in faith until the day when the promised land of Canaan would be their own. (See Genesis 24:2–8 for Abraham's insistence that there could be no going back once God's promise had been received.)

A better country

In this determined stance of the patriarchs, Hebrews finds a model for Christian discipleship. Christians too are people who have left behind a settled and secure life to enter a pilgrimage of faith. They too have the opportunity to return if they so wish, but they must not even consider such an option any more than Abraham did. For they too are looking forward, seeking a homeland. And that homeland is not a piece of earthly territory between the Mediterranean Sea and the Jordan, but an even 'better country', a heavenly one (v. 16).

This is the same idea that was developed in chapter 4, of a heavenly 'rest' still awaiting God's faithful people. In that chapter the idea was based on the story of Joshua and the eventual conquest of Canaan, in fulfilment of God's promises to the patriarchs. Our 'rest', our promised land, however, is in heaven. We are, as Paul reminds us, 'citizens of heaven' (Philippians 3:20), and so remain aliens here on earth.

The city

The nomadic life is not the final goal. Abraham looked forward to 'the city that has foundations' (v. 10), and God will honour the faithful pilgrimage of his nomad people by bringing them at last to 'a city'. For many people today this seems a rather unattractive prospect: earthly cities too easily turn into places of squalor and vice, and modern urbanites dream of escaping to the countryside. But for the nomad, a city is the essence of stability, of being finally 'at home'. So at the end of the Bible it is with the promise of a heavenly city, the new Jerusalem, that the vision reaches its climax, and in that city God himself will dwell among his faithful people in perfect happiness (Revelation 21:3–4).

FOR REFLECTION

Does this old spiritual give us a right model for understanding our situation as Christian disciples?

This world is not my home;
I'm just a-passing through.
My treasures are laid up
Somewhere beyond the blue.
The Saviour beckons me
From heaven's open door,
And I can't feel at home
In this world any more.

87 HEBREWS 11:17–22

MORE *about the* PATRIARCHS

The sacrifice of Isaac

Before the summary passage in 11:13–16, we heard of God's promise to Abraham of a son in his old age, of the faith that took such an unlikely promise seriously, and of how the promise was in fact fulfilled in the countless descendants of Abraham. But there was a time when it looked as if the promise had been revoked. So we return now to Abraham, to remember the greatest test which his faith had to face (Genesis 22:1–19).

For Abraham, everything now depended on Isaac. The future to which he had so persistently looked forward was bound up in this precious young man. So to be ordered to kill him as a sacrifice must have seemed a cruel joke. Not only was human sacrifice repugnant in itself, and the sacrifice of his own son even more unthinkable, but it was all his hopes and all the promises of God that would be killed along with his son. Surely God could not really mean it?

That is the way we think, but in the Genesis story Abraham gives no hint of scepticism. He did what he was told (until he was prevented at the last minute), and our author says that he did it in faith—not just a blind faith that somehow God must know best, but a resurrection faith. For Abraham, death, even the death of his son and heir, was not the end, and could not frustrate God's promise. Perhaps he reflected on how his own 'deadness' (11:12) had been no barrier to God's purpose. Of course, in the event, Isaac was rescued, and there was no need for a physical resurrection, but for the author of Hebrews his return from the brink of death is almost the same thing. Abraham's 'resurrection faith' was vindicated.

Patriarchal blessings

Blessings conveyed by father to son(s) play a prominent role in the Genesis stories, and for our author they are another pointer to a faith which could see beyond the immediate circumstances to God's promised future. The famous story of Isaac's blessings on Jacob and Esau (Genesis 27) strikes us first and foremost as a story of selfish trickery, but underlying it is the conviction that the father's blessing, however obtained, is irrevocable, and that what he has pronounced must certainly be fulfilled. It is thus another indication of a faith which can see things that are as yet invisible.

A similar power is found in Jacob's lengthy blessings on his own sons (Genesis 49), and on his grandsons Ephraim and Manasseh (Genesis 48). The blessing of the sons of Joseph, like Isaac's blessing of his two sons, reverses the normal expectation that the older will be the more important. So Jacob, like his father, could see in advance that God's purpose was to overturn the natural order, and this 'faith' was vindicated.

Looking forward

For Abraham, Isaac and Jacob, then, 'faith' meant a firm grasp on the reality of God's promises and purpose, however paradoxical they might seem to normal human sight. It was for them 'the assurance of things hoped for, the conviction of things not seen'. And what faith made real to them, history was to prove true.

It is Joseph's deathbed words (Genesis 50:24–25), like those of his father and grandfather, that our author also records, rather than any of the extraordinary achievements of his own lifetime. He too died looking forward. His faith could see beyond the immediate prosperity of Egypt to the time when their refuge would become a prison, and the land which God had promised to Abraham would again become their goal. So his last words were to ensure that his bones would not be left in Egypt, but would rejoin his ancestors in Canaan, where God's purpose for his people was to ripen towards its promised fulfilment. Thus he too, like his ancestors, 'died in faith without having received the promises', but having seen and greeted them from afar (v. 13).

PRAYER

Lord, give us the faith to look beyond the discouraging circumstances in which we may find ourselves, and to take a firm hold on the good things you have promised. Amen.

From EGYPT *to the* PROMISED LAND

The story of faith in action resumes with Moses and the return from Egypt (which Joseph had looked forward to), and continues into the time of his successor Joshua, when the promise to Abraham began to be fulfilled in the conquest of the promised land.

Moses—a child of faith

No doubt the decision of Moses' parents to protect their child from Pharaoh's 'ethnic cleansing' (Exodus 1:22—2:10) was a thoroughly natural instinct, but our author sees in it also the mark of faith, in that, whether they knew it or not, they were preserving the future deliverer of Israel and so making it possible for God's purpose, as yet unrevealed, to be fulfilled. And like their son later (v. 27), they were willing to defy the power of Pharaoh, because they paid more heed to their unseen God than to the immediate threat of human retribution.

Moses' choice

Moses himself admirably fulfils our author's specifications for a hero of faith. Like his ancestors, he opted not for the easy life but for the harder road which would lead to the fulfilment of God's promises. His fortuitous royal upbringing entitled him to a life of human influence and luxury among the treasures of Egypt, but to have accepted that role would have been for him the 'pleasures of sin' (v. 25) because it would have been to turn his back on the special role for which God had prepared him. Such pleasure would in any case have been only 'fleeting', whereas it was by the way of ill-treatment and abuse that the true and lasting 'reward' would be found. (By popping in the anachronistic mention of 'the Christ' in verse 26, the author drops a broad hint as to where his readers are to find a parallel in their own situation.)

Similarly, Moses' defiance of Pharaoh stemmed from the ability to see beyond the immediate threat to the more ultimate sovereignty of God. Moses thus illustrates powerfully the twin perspective of faith set out in verse 1, the 'looking forward' and the 'looking up': his 'looking ahead to the reward' demonstrates 'the assurance of things hoped for', and his 'seeing him who is invisible' echoes 'the conviction of things not seen'.

The triumphs of faith

The stirring events of the exodus and conquest provide an abundance of further examples, from which the author chooses four more.

The Passover sprinkling of blood demonstrates Moses' confidence in God's promise that when the angel of death visited the firstborn in Egypt, he would spare the houses marked with this blood (Exodus 12:1–13). The Red Sea provided another similarly remarkable escape by equally improbable means (Exodus 14), and the fall of the impregnable walls of Jericho was not to human strength but as the result of a bizarre action which only the obedience of faith could have expected to have any effect (Joshua 6:1–20).

Each of these 'successes' against all the odds depended on Moses and Joshua, and the rest of the people following their lead, believing God's words and acting on that belief, even though any rational calculation would have declared the proposed actions to be absurd. In each case we see 'the assurance of things hoped for' writ large, and coupled with it the practical willingness to stake their safety and their future on that assurance.

The final example is not on the same grand scale, but even the humble prostitute of Jericho, foreigner as she was, found that when she trusted the word of the God of Israel he did not let her down (Joshua 2:1–21; 6:25). Faith is willing to stake everything on the reliability of God and his promises.

FOR REFLECTION

These stories of stirring events in Israel's history seem far away from our everyday world. Where in our own experience and circumstances can we find similar challenges to faith?

89 HEBREWS 11:32–40

STILL LOOKING FORWARD

Our author's potted history of the triumphs of faith in Old Testament Israel has still reached only to the beginning of their life in the promised land. But he has made his point, and it is up to his readers now to take the story further by drawing on what they know of the Old Testament stories. To help them in this, he provides a list of names of further heroes who would have been included if time had allowed, though this list too gets us no further than David, still fully a thousand years in the past. But a further general reference to 'the prophets' (v. 32) points the way into the later centuries of Israel's history.

The triumphs of faith

In verses 33–38 we hear of some of the typical achievements of these men and women of faith, mostly in fairly generalized terms which could apply to a number of different historical figures, but in a few cases with a more recognizable reference to a particular individual. Thus we meet, apparently, Daniel who 'shut the mouths of lions' (Daniel 6), Shadrach, Meshach and Abednego who 'quenched raging fire' (Daniel 3), and Isaiah who, according to tradition, was 'sawn in two' by the orders of King Manasseh. The women who 'received their dead by resurrection' are probably the widow of Zarephath (1 Kings 17:8–24) and the woman of Shunem (2 Kings 4:8–37), whose sons were restored to life through the prayers of Elijah and Elisha respectively—in their case the faith seems to be more that of the prophets concerned than of the women themselves.

This is a corporate portrait of those to whom God and his promises are more real and more important than adverse circumstances and human opposition, however immediate and intense. Many of them belong to the 'noble army of martyrs', for it is noteworthy that the author does not speak of all of them being delivered from persecution and death. In this world they allowed themselves to be humiliated, tormented and killed rather than renounce their loyalty to the one true God. In this they were models to be followed by the readers of this letter in their vulnerable position.

'Of whom the world was not worthy'

The reason why they were able to remain faithful through such experiences was 'the assurance of things hoped for' and 'the conviction of things not seen' (11:1). That is why they 'refused to accept release, in order to obtain a better resurrection' (v. 35). People of faith are those for whom the world to come is as real as or even more real than this world, and who can therefore sit light to this world's values and even to life itself.

The world is not worthy of such people. This striking phrase in verse 38 is the more remarkable when you read it in its context, which describes what the world would regard as losers, those 'despised and rejected' by other people, and whose way of life (and of death) would be the object of pity rather than of envy. But in the eyes of faith these are the people to be congratulated. They have found the secret of true life.

Something better

But there is a twist in the tail of this great panorama of Old Testament faith. All these great men and women—even the all-time greats, Abraham and Moses—magnificent as their faith was, still had something missing (vv. 39–40). They were still looking forward, and the ultimate fulfilment of God's promises remained for them still 'unseen'. That time of fulfilment would not come until 'these last days' when God would send his Son (1:2). 'Perfection', the final outworking of God's redemptive purpose, must wait until that time.

But now it has come! And it is the incredible privilege of the writer and his readers to be the people of those last days. Only with 'us' is the pattern completed, and all that Abraham and the patriarchs, Moses and Joshua and all the heroes of this chapter had looked forward to is finally achieved. 'We' are the final piece in the jigsaw.

And these Jewish Christians were thinking of giving *that* up!

PRAYER

Forgive us, Lord, for the shortsightedness which can see only the problems of the life of faith, and help us to recognize the privilege of being caught up in the fulfilment of your age-long plan of salvation. Amen.

90 HEBREWS 12:1–2

Racing *to the* Finish

The long and exhilarating celebration of 'faith' in chapter 11 was not written just as interesting history. It was designed to reinforce the challenge to the readers in 10:35–39 not to give up their allegiance to Christ, but to press on in faith, whatever the cost. Now, at the beginning of chapter 12, the message is driven home.

In the arena

The imagery is of a great sports stadium, in which they (we) are entered in a long-distance race. In the stands around them are a 'great cloud of witnesses'—banks of eager spectators urging them on. The Christian life is not a solitary pursuit: it is uncomfortably public, and to fail to complete the race would be not just a personal disappointment but a public disgrace.

But the spectators are not just any old crowd of armchair critics, free with advice and barracking but not willing to run themselves. No, the 'great cloud of witnesses' are the heroes of faith whom we have celebrated in chapter 11. They have already run the race themselves, and finished their course with honour. Now they sit in the stands and cheer on their successors, and to those who are losing heart they cry out from their own experience, 'Go on: it's worth it!'

In the London Marathon there are serious competitors and fun-runners. It isn't difficult to spot the difference. No one who wants to compete seriously runs wearing an elephant's head or carrying a tray of glasses. And the Christian life is a serious race. Unnecessary weights will get in the way, and tolerated sin will hold us back like weeds wrapped round our legs. Like the soldier Paul talked about in 2 Timothy 2:4, we cannot afford to get 'entangled' in anything which holds us back from the demanding course of discipleship.

Looking to Jesus

Successful running of the race demands not only single-minded determination, but also a clear vision of the goal. And the goal is, in a word, Jesus. So the Christian runner should not be distracted by the immediate things in the foreground but must 'look *away* (which is what the Greek word literally means) to Jesus'. Jesus himself is the key to our life of faith, and that for two reasons which are summed up in the words 'the pioneer and perfecter of our faith'.

He is the 'pioneer' (compare 'pioneer of our salvation' in 2:10) because he himself has already run the race before us. As such, he is the latest and most glorious in the long line of heroes we have traced through chapter 11, the supreme example of living by faith. He was able to face up to the suffering of the cross, and especially the 'shame' which such a public and humiliating form of execution brought, because of 'the joy set before him'. Here we see 'the assurance of things hoped for' writ large. So Jesus has won through, and now he enjoys the 'reward' of his seat at God's right hand.

But Jesus is more than a great example of faith and perseverance. From his seat beside the throne of God he offers not only a model for our life of faith, but also the resources to make it successful. There he 'always lives to make intercession for us' (7:25), and so we have the supreme authority in the universe on our side. That is why he is not only the pioneer but also the 'perfecter' of our faith. He makes it work. So we run the race not in our own inadequate strength but in his.

FOR REFLECTION

Consider these two verses as a 'nutshell' guide to living the Christian life. What are their key themes concerning (a) the incentives and (b) the means to successful Christian discipleship?

91 HEBREWS 12:3–6

A POSITIVE VIEW *of* SUFFERING

Our author is writing to people who have already had to suffer as a result of their Christian faith, and who may well be called to suffer more. He is afraid that they may not be able to cope with this, and may be tempted rather to give up their Christian profession. So in these verses he tries to help them to see their suffering for the faith in a more positive light, particularly by drawing their attention to a remarkable passage from the book of Proverbs.

Jesus as the example of godly suffering

The reference to the cross and its shame in 12:2 leads the author to compare his readers' situation with that of their 'pioneer'. If Jesus suffered willingly in fulfilling his mission, should not they also be prepared to do so? If they were experiencing 'hostility from sinners' (v. 3), so also did he. Indeed he became the focus of all the hatred of those who were threatened by his teaching and example, and it took him to the cross. But they have not yet 'resisted to the point of shedding your blood' (v. 4). Of course that may yet happen; they would not be the first Christian martyrs. But even if it comes to that, they will be doing no more than following where their master has already gone.

Seen in that light, suffering for the faith becomes not a meaningless and negative experience, but a sharing with their Lord. By 'looking away to Jesus', therefore, they can put their own lesser sufferings into perspective, so that they will not be demoralized by them but rather overcome them through the faith which can see through to the 'joy set before them'.

The discipline of the Lord

So suffering with Christ may even come to be seen as a privilege. But the author here goes further: it can also be understood as positively beneficial, when it is interpreted in the light of God's fatherly care.

Here we enter an area with which much modern thought has little sympathy. The old days of 'Spare the rod and spoil the child' are fading fast. Physical punishment is frowned on, and discipline in any form is an unpopular concept. To think of parenthood in terms of authority and discipline seems increasingly old-fashioned. And to apply the concept of discipline specifically to suffering seems particularly regrettable.

So the words of Proverbs 3:11–12 which are quoted here in verses 5 and 6 are a challenge to some modern values. They assume that 'punishment' has a good purpose, and that discipline is the basis of education. But these words are set neither in the prison nor in the classroom, but firmly in the home, as the primary place of 'education'. They understand the discipline which God exercises over his 'children' as an expression of his love. The ones who are 'chastised' (the Greek word is literally 'flogged'!) are his own beloved children, 'the son in whom he delights'. The discipline is a measure of the father's love and care.

It is important to note that by interpreting his readers' suffering in the light of the concept of fatherly discipline in Proverbs, the author is tracing their sufferings to the hand of God rather than to the more immediate cause of their human opponents. This robust sense of God's ultimate control over all that happens to his people is characteristic of the biblical writers. What we might regard as the result of accident or of human malice is, for them, taken up into the all-embracing purpose of a loving and disciplining God. And in that broader perspective it is not meaningless, and must not be taken lightly. Rather, as the following verses will explain, the 'discipline of the Lord' is imposed for our ultimate good.

Such a view of Christian suffering needs to be expressed and applied with great care, if it is not either to descend to the level of Pollyanna platitude or to be grossly insensitive to real human affliction. Suffering and pain are not good in themselves, and much of our suffering defies simple explanation as 'divine discipline'. Our author is not offering a global theology of evil which 'explains' earthquakes or cancer or the Battle of the Somme. He is putting his readers' suffering discipleship into perspective by setting it within the loving purpose of a Father who plans the best for his children. Here, as always, it is important to read one passage in the light of the whole biblical message, not on its own.

PRAYER

Loving Father, help us your children to trust you even when you discipline us, and to trace your good purpose when the way of discipleship is hard. Amen.

Parental Discipline

Having introduced his striking quotation from Proverbs, our author now goes on to draw out its meaning and its relevance to the difficult situation in which his readers found themselves.

God's true children

The Greek word which is translated 'discipline' in these verses is also used more generally for 'education' or 'upbringing'. It is a parent's chief concern that the child should be brought up well, and should become an adult to be proud of. And prominent among the factors which go to make up that process of 'education' is discipline, in the sense of correcting what is wrong. To shrink from practising discipline is to abandon your parental responsibility and to show that you do not ultimately care for the child's good.

So the experience of discipline is a mark of being a true child of God. To be left to our own devices, untaught and uncorrected, would show that God did not care for us, that we were not his true children. Of course no one enjoys being disciplined, but when that discipline is seen in its proper context of parental love, it can be seen as a positive and indeed necessary experience. That is why the true child of God can be content to 'endure trials' (v. 7), knowing that they are part of God's loving process of education.

Discipline—human and divine

When we talk about God as our 'Father' we are using a metaphor from human relationships, and there is always the danger that some people's human experience of fatherhood may not be a happy one, so that for them the image can be less than helpful. But this passage assumes that our experience of earthly parents has been a healthy one. In such a relationship there is discipline, but also respect and trust. We realize, later if not at the time, that the discipline which we disliked was imposed with good motives and for our own ultimate good, and so we do not resent it. How much more, then, when the 'disciplinarian' is the 'Father of spirits' (that is, our 'spiritual Father') whose love and wisdom are beyond question (v. 9)?

Human parents can make mistakes, and sometimes the discipline which they think to be for the best is misguided. It may even be imposed for selfish motives (though that is not necessarily the implication of 'as seemed best to them', v. 10). But God's discipline is 'for our own good'. Its purpose is to enable us to grow up to be like our Father, by 'sharing his holiness' (v. 10). Holiness is a word which sums up the distinctive character of God himself, but ever since Old Testament days he has called on his people to be like him: 'You shall be holy as I am holy' (Leviticus 19:2; 20:26). Such a goal is worth some discipline on the way!

Putting suffering in perspective

If the suffering which comes to us as followers of Jesus is understood in this light, it is no longer a purely negative experience, however unpleasant it may be at the time. There are, we are often told, 'no gains without pains'. That is why athletes submit to what in any other context might be described as simple torture, and mountain climbers push themselves to the limits of endurance in order to reach the summit. The 'assurance of things hoped for' (11:1) makes it all worth while. And the goal of our discipline is 'the peaceful fruit of righteousness' (v. 11), a pregnant phrase which spells out perhaps something of what it means to grow into sharing God's holiness. And isn't that a far better prospect than going through our lives as spiritual spoilt brats?

FOR REFLECTION

As we noted at the end of the last study, there are limits to how far this 'disciplinary' view of suffering can be used to account for all life's unpleasant experiences and apparent unfairness. The author of this passage was talking apparently about suffering which might come to his readers as a result of remaining faithful to their Christian commitment.

How, if at all, may this insight be used to help those who face suffering in their own circumstances, health, or relationships, which is not obviously attributable to their Christian discipleship? How far do you find that it can throw light on your own sufferings?

93

PRESSING ON

After a brief comment on the *theory* of suffering (as 'the discipline of the Lord'), the author now returns to his main pastoral purpose, to strengthen the resolve of his readers to keep going in their Christian race, however difficult the going may become.

Running straight

Verse 12 sounds like unfit runners at the end of the London Marathon, with sagging arms and buckling knees, wobbling from exhaustion. But they are not yet at the end of the race. This is no time for giving in to tiredness and discouragement, but rather for a second wind and for setting themselves more firmly on course for the finish. 'Make straight paths for your feet' echoes the Greek text of Proverbs 4:26, part of a general exhortation to single-minded and purposeful living, not deviating from the path of God's will, but running forward with 'your gaze straight before you' (Proverbs 4:25).

The athletic metaphor continues in the second half of verse 13. The focus may be on the runner's own fitness, not allowing a strained limb to be dislocated and so put you out of the race. In that case it is a call to spiritual vigilance, to keeping yourself in the peak of condition for the life of faith. But the verb is more literally 'be turned out of the way', and it is possible that the author is thinking here not of the individual runner's concern for their own success, but of a team race, in which one runner's staggering may knock another who is already struggling ('lame') out of the race altogether. If you fail, you may have a disastrous effect on your vulnerable fellow disciples as well. Certainly the following verses focus not so much on individual godliness as on the spiritual health of the whole Christian group.

Peace with holiness

Our author now spells out some of the aspects of spiritual 'fitness' which he sees as important in his readers' situation. First comes 'peace with everyone' (v. 14). He may be thinking especially of good relations within the disciple community, but his words are more comprehensive than that, and would include also their persecutors, in the spirit of Jesus' command to 'love your enemies' (Matthew 5:44), and Paul's exhortation to 'live peaceably with all' (Romans 12:18). The call to 'pursue' peace goes further than a mere avoidance of conflict; it is an active policy, energetically undertaken. Blessed are the peace*makers*.

There is another echo of Jesus' Beatitudes also in the next phrase, 'the holiness without which no one will see the Lord'. It is those who are 'pure in heart' who will 'see God', said Jesus (Matthew 5:8). 'Holiness', as we have just seen in 12:10, is God's own character, and only those who share it can be with him. That is why God's people as a community are called to 'be holy, as he is holy' (Leviticus 19:2).

The root of bitterness

One person who goes wrong can affect the others. An individual who falls short of God's gracious purpose can become a 'root of bitterness' (v. 15) which, like one root of nettle buried in a garden, can in time overrun the whole plot. So the unspiritual and self-centred attitude and actions of such a person can infect the whole community and 'knock it off course' in its progress towards the goal of holiness. Hence the call for vigilance ('See to it': literally 'keeping watch', 'overseeing') not only over one's own spiritual health but over that of one's fellow Christians, so that no such weeds develop.

The shortsightedness of Esau, who cared more for his immediate hunger than for his status and responsibilities as the elder son (Genesis 25:29–34), illustrates the danger of taking your eyes off the goal, and giving in to present circumstances. Not only does this incident mark him out as 'immoral and godless', but our author reminds his readers of what happened to Esau subsequently: he lost the blessing reserved for the firstborn, and despite his agonized attempts to get it back, it was too late (Genesis 27:30–40). The moral is obvious: don't miss out on God's promises by a short-sighted capitulation to pressure, or you too may find that there is no way back. Verses 25–29 will hammer the message home.

PRAYER

Give me courage when the world is rough.
Keep me loving when the world is tough;
Leap and sing in all I do,
Keep me travelling along with you.

Sydney Carter (b. 1915)

HEBREWS 12:18–24

A TALE *of* TWO MOUNTAINS

The recurrent theme of this letter is that what we have in Christ is far better than what went before in the Old Testament. In these verses, this theme comes to graphic expression in the contrast between Mount Sinai, the terrible mountain at which Israel's national unity was forged, and Mount Zion which represents the heavenly Jerusalem, the home of God's true people of the new covenant. To give up their Christian pilgrimage now would be to go back to the terrors of Sinai, and to miss the joys of Zion.

Sinai—mountain of fear

The vivid description of Sinai is drawn from Exodus 19, where God's presence at the holy mountain was experienced in dramatic but frightening sights and sounds and in words of dire warning. Even though they had come to the holy mountain of God, they were made sharply aware that God himself remained at a distance. It was a mountain that 'could be touched' (an earthly scenario as opposed to the heavenly Jerusalem) but yet it must not be touched on pain of death. Even Moses, the one man permitted to climb the mountain in order to meet with God and receive his law, was terrified. That, our author implies, is what the old covenant was like—a covenant of distance and of fear in the presence of an awesome God.

Zion—mountain of celebration

To come to Sinai was only to be kept at arm's length, but to come to Zion is to be welcomed and included. It is no less truly a holy mountain, for this is where the 'living God' (v. 22) himself is found. But here, it seems, unlike at Sinai, he is holding open house. The earthly Mount Zion (Jerusalem and its temple) was the place of pilgrimage, where the people of Israel gathered for festivals, but now we are shown its heavenly counterpart, and it is the place for all God's people, not only for Israel.

The description of the various groups who make up the heavenly gathering paints a picture of the party to end all parties. The innumerable angels are 'in festal gathering', a word used for special celebrations. Here too are assembled all the 'firstborn' (v. 23), probably a term for redeemed humanity who follow Jesus, himself the 'Firstborn' *par excellence* (1:6). Together with them we find the 'spirits of the righteous made perfect', probably those heroes of faith who at the end of chapter 11 we found still awaiting their 'perfection' until Christ came (11:39–40). And the host of this festive gathering is of course God himself, the judge of all, by whose just decree these people have been 'enrolled in heaven', while beside him is the one whose unique self-sacrifice has made it all possible—Jesus, the mediator of a new covenant which makes for ever obsolete the old covenant of fear set up at Mount Sinai.

Along with this impressive list of the participants in the heavenly festivities, it is surprising to meet also 'the sprinkled blood' (v. 24). But this too is part of the contrast. It was by the sprinkling of blood that the first covenant at Sinai was ratified (Exodus 24:5–8), and the new covenant too has its sacrifice, as chapters 9 and 10 have spelled out at length. But whereas blood normally calls for vengeance, as did the blood of Abel (Genesis 4:10), this blood has a better message as it calls for the forgiveness of those who acknowledge Jesus as their high priest.

'You have come to Mount Zion'

Our author is not setting before his readers something new and strange. This is where they already belong. They are citizens of heaven, and invited guests at the heavenly party. And yet it is this incalculable privilege which they are in danger of giving up, and for what? For the terrors of Sinai! It is time to come to their senses, and to see things from the perspective of heaven, to regain 'the assurance of things hoped for, the conviction of things not seen'.

FOR REFLECTION

Many of the favourite hymns of the Victorians focused on the hope of heaven ('Jerusalem the Golden', for example), but they seem to be less popular these days. Does this say something important about their understanding of the Christian life—and ours?

95 HEBREWS 12:25–29

ONE LAST WARNING

The enormity of the contrast between the privilege his readers now have in Christ and the prospect of what would face them if they were to give it all up provokes the author to yet another, and this time final, warning about the dangers of falling away. The theme has run through the whole letter, but has come to the fore especially in 2:1–4; 3:7—4:13; 6:4–8 and 10:26–31. In one sense he has nothing new to add here, but these verses, with their suggestive echo of the 'shaking of the heavens and the earth' in Haggai 2:6, provide an impressive rhetorical climax.

The voice of God

At Sinai the people found God's presence so terrifying that they begged that he would not speak to them any more (12:19; compare Exodus 20:19). Exodus 19:18 mentions that the mountain quaked, and the author links this with the power of God's voice. It was fear that made them 'refuse the one who was speaking' (v. 25) at that time, but as time went on, their refusal extended to disobedience to God's words. As we have been forcefully reminded in 3:7—4:13, they did not escape the consequences of that 'hardening of their hearts' (Psalm 95:8), but died in the wilderness and never attained the promised 'rest' (Psalm 95:11).

In Israel's refusal to listen to God, the author finds a paradigm for his readers' danger of 'neglecting so great a salvation' (2:3). But for them the stakes are still higher. The God whose voice then shook an earthly mountain speaks now from heaven, and according to Haggai's prophecy (Haggai 2:6), when God acts in the last days it is not only the earth which is to be shaken but even heaven itself.

Haggai's prophecy is of the 'shaking' of heaven and earth and of all nations so that the treasures of all the nations may be brought in to fill his house in Jerusalem with glory. He was thinking, apparently, of the future splendour of the earthly Mount Zion, but in his words our author finds a pointer also to the heavenly Zion, that new and everlasting Zion to which the way has now been opened as we saw in the previous section. So the time has come for the final shaking of earth and heaven. This is no time for refusing to listen to God's powerful voice: 'How much less will we escape!' (v. 25).

An unshakeable kingdom

In the 'shaking' of heaven and earth, the author of this letter finds a pointer to their impermanence. All created things can be 'shaken', so that one day they will be removed altogether. When that happens, only what is unshakeable will remain, and it is an 'unshakeable kingdom' that God has made available to his people through the coming of Jesus.

The 'kingdom of God' has not been a prominent theme of Hebrews, as it is of Jesus' own teaching in the Synoptic Gospels, but in 1:8 the author has quoted the psalm which speaks of the Messiah's everlasting kingdom, and the frequent references to Jesus sitting at God's right hand convey the same idea. As his people, we belong to that unshakeable kingdom, the one place of security when the world falls apart.

Taking God seriously

So we have every reason to give thanks to God for this great salvation. But our gratitude must be tinged with awe. The God whose voice shook Sinai is still to be treated with 'reverence and awe' (v. 28), not with easy familiarity. Only so can we offer 'acceptable worship'. God is not to be trifled with, for, as the Sinai imagery of Exodus 19 has so forcefully reminded us, he is a 'consuming fire' (the actual phrase is drawn from Deuteronomy 4:24). To refuse to listen to such a God would be unthinkable, for 'it is a fearful thing to fall into the hands of the living God' (10:31).

PRAYER

'Today if you hear his voice, do not harden your hearts.'
(Hebrews 3:7–8; Psalm 95:7–8)

Lord, may we heed this warning, and give you the honour which is your due, not only in our thoughts and worship, but in our commitment and obedience to your will. Amen.

96

ANGELS UNAWARES

The tone of the letter now changes as we come to the concluding paragraphs. After the sustained argument and sophisticated biblical explorations of the previous chapters, this last chapter has rather a 'bitty' feel. A wide range of subjects are touched on quite briefly, sometimes without any very clear connection with what has gone before. The author has made his main point, and now concludes with a series of pastoral exhortations and greetings, so that for the first time this book begins to sound more like a typical New Testament letter, and less like an extended sermon.

Hospitality

The first three verses touch on three aspects of the concern for one another which should be the mark of the people of God. (Remember Jesus' last commandment in John 13:34–35, to 'love one another', with the comment, 'By this everyone will know that you are my disciples.')

Verse 1 is the most general, calling for 'mutual love'. The Greek word is *philadelphia*, 'brotherly love', the affection and concern which members of a family have for one another. While of course Christians are called to love all people, even our enemies, there is a special relationship with those who are our 'brothers and sisters' in the faith, and it is that mutual love which the author specially commends (as he has already in different words in 10:24–25).

But to focus only on *philadelphia* would be too cosy. We are also called to hospitality, *philoxenia*, literally 'love of strangers'. Perhaps he is thinking of visiting Christians from other churches (and if this group of Jewish Christians were in Rome, such visitors might be quite frequent), but he does not restrict *philoxenia* only to members of the Christian community; the possibility of 'entertaining angels without knowing it' (v. 2) suggests that he had in mind people who came with no letters of commendation. The intriguing phrase is derived from the experience of Abraham in Genesis 18, when he welcomed and entertained three 'men' who appeared outside his tent, only to discover later that they were angels (Genesis 19:1) sent on a divine mission, one of whom is apparently identified as 'the Lord' himself

(Genesis 18:13, 22). Even if in less dramatic ways, many can testify to the unexpected blessings which have come from welcoming strangers into their homes.

Thirdly, because this is a church under persecution, they are reminded specifically of those undergoing imprisonment and torture (v. 3), very likely members of their own group (compare 10:32–34), though again the author does not restrict it. To speak of 'remembering' such people in a context of mutual love and hospitality is surely to call for more than kind thoughts or even prayers. In a prison in the ancient world, the very necessities of life would often depend on provisions being brought in by family and friends, not to mention the basic need for human companionship. The basis for such necessary support is to be not just philanthropy from a comfortable distance, but that practical empathy which should be a characteristic of members of the body of Christ (1 Corinthians 12:26).

Marriage

Verse 4 stands on its own, and we have no clue as to any special circumstances which may have caused the author to include this uncompromising reminder of the Christian code of married fidelity. But the New Testament provides plenty of evidence that the sexual ethics of the first-century Roman world were a constant threat to Christian marriage, and Paul often had to remind his churches that God has called us to a higher standard, so that what may be 'normal' in the world around is not therefore to be tolerated in the Church. The situation is not very different in our world today, and the simple demands of verse 4 remain a vital reminder to us of what God expects among his own people.

PRAYER

Lord, help us to love one another, not only in word but in deed. Amen.

HEBREWS 13:5–8

TRUSTING GOD

God and Mammon

Jesus warned his disciples of the competition which could occur between loyalty to God and concern for material security (Matthew 6:24–33). It is not that money is evil in itself, but that whereas it should be a slave it can easily usurp the place of master. So what we are warned about here is not 'money' but 'love of money', just as Paul declared in 1 Timothy 6:10 that 'the love of money is a root of all kinds of evil' (see comments in Study 20).

When our author goes on to ask his readers to 'be content with what you have' (echoing Paul's principle set out in Philippians 4: 11–12), he assumes that they have enough to live on. What he is concerned about is the corrosive effect of the constant desire for more, and that has not changed. Indeed, as the world has become more sophisticated, it seems to breed greater and greater discontent. We live, as John V. Taylor so memorably reminded us in his passionate book *Enough is Enough* (SCM Press, 1975), in a culture of Excess, and in such a culture the first casualty is contentment.

Instead, our trust should be in God the provider, and the author underlines this basic sense of security with two Old Testament quotations, one taken from God's reassuring words to Joshua as he launched out into the unknown territory of the promised land with all the formidable strength of its Canaanite occupants (Joshua 1:5; compare Deuteronomy 31:6, 8), the other from Psalm 118:6 celebrating the 'steadfast love' of the Lord which overcomes all human opposition. The situation of the readers of this letter (and our own) might not be as dramatic as those of Joshua and the psalmist, but the Lord who can be trusted in such extreme circumstances can surely be relied on for the necessities of life.

'Your leaders'

The same term will recur in 13:17 and 24. As we noted in the Introduction, this is the only term in this letter for any sort of office-bearers within the church, and it is very broad and unspecific. Beyond a general role of leadership, we simply do not know what they did or what more particular title of office they may (or may not) have had. In 13:17 and 24 the term clearly refers to those still holding responsibility within the community, but here (v. 7) the call to 'remember', the fact that 'spoke' is in the past tense, and the mention of the 'outcome' of their lives, all point rather to those who have already died, perhaps especially to those through whose witness this church was first set up.

Such people are to be remembered with honour, and their lives and work to be an example for those who follow on. 'Imitation' is a frequent theme in the New Testament: we learn by example as well as by teaching. It is the awesome responsibility of those who 'lead' (and few of us do not in some small sphere at least) to leave a suitable model for others to copy.

Yesterday and today and for ever

The 'leaders', it seems, have died, and it is only by memory that their help may now be obtained. But it is not so with Jesus, the 'pioneer and perfecter of our faith' (12:2). He is not just a memory but a present Lord, who 'always lives to make intercession for us' (7:25). That is why he, rather than the transient possession of money, is the secure basis for our faith.

In such ways this famous slogan fits appropriately into the context of the verses which precede it. But of course its relevance is far broader than that. The epigrammatic form of verse 8 (there is no verb in the Greek) suggests a 'motto' which our early Christian forebears carried around in their heads as a constant resource in the multifarious pressures of living for Jesus in a changing and often unsympathetic world. It can serve us no less powerfully as such, now that their today is our yesterday, and their tomorrow is our today.

PRAYER

Thank you, Lord Jesus Christ, for your unchanging love and power.
As our world changes, and we ourselves change, may we remain
secure in your unchangeableness. Amen.

OUTSIDE *the* CAMP

Within a chapter of apparently disconnected short sections, these verses provide the one rather more sustained argument and development of a theme. And here again the writer reverts to his favourite style of argument, drawing attention to details from Old Testament texts and using them as a basis for drawing a contrast between the old and the new. As he does so, we are reminded of a number of themes from earlier in this letter, as we shall see. The section begins with some thoughts about food.

Getting things in perspective

The exhortation to beware of 'all kinds of strange teachings' (v. 9) is very general, but the sentence goes on to a more specific subject, food-laws, and it is likely that the 'strange teachings' our author had in mind were in this area. The Jewish food-laws were a constant source of tension in the early Church, especially because, if properly observed, they made it practically impossible for Jewish and Gentile Christians to eat together. Jesus himself raised eyebrows by his radical teaching about what does and does not defile (Mark 7:1–23), and Paul frequently had to return to the issue, opposing those who, even after the church leaders in Jerusalem had debated the question (Acts 15), continued to try to compel Christians, even Gentile Christians, to adopt the Levitical code of 'clean food'.

The author does not want his readers distracted with such disputes. It is better to be strengthened by *grace* than by food-laws—a simple, uncomplicated, and surely unanswerable riposte! There are more important matters.

The alternative altar

The thought of ritual cleanness in matters of food leads our author on to a further thought about food and ritual. The worship of those who observe the Levitical laws was focused on the tabernacle and its purity. Those who no longer follow the Levitical rules cannot approach its altar. But, says our author, they have no need to, because now there is an alternative altar, set up apart from the Levitical sanctuary. He is thinking probably of the 'heavenly tabernacle' where Christ, the one true priest, now officiates (8:1–6; 9:11–12, 24–26). That is where 'we' belong, and the priests of the old covenant have no place there.

The thought of being outside the tabernacle leads him to a further biblical reflection. 'Outside' was where the bodies of sacrificial animals were taken to be burned after their blood had been offered in the sanctuary on the Day of Atonement (Leviticus 16:27)—and it was 'outside the city gate' (v. 12) that Christ also was taken to be slaughtered for our sins. He was rejected by the religious establishment, just as the readers of the letter find themselves kept 'outside' by the non-Christian Jewish establishment of their day. There is therefore now a deep divide between the old and the new, between the official tabernacle with its 'clean' food and Jesus and his followers, rejected as unclean, but through his sacrificial blood brought into a new and better relationship with God—'outside the camp', but with an altar and a sacrifice that make the old system obsolete and worthless.

Going out with Jesus

'Outside' is the place of ostracism and abuse, but if that was what Jesus suffered, they must not be ashamed to join him 'outside'. And that is where a pilgrim people belong, as chapter 11 has so vividly illustrated. The tabernacle and the 'camp' of which it is the centre (the author continues to think in wilderness terms) are not their true home. Rather, like Abraham and the patriarchs, they are looking for the new and better city which God has promised. To be obliged to leave the old order behind is no penalty when they have something so much better in store.

These verses, then, in the rather quaint language of the Old Testament sacrificial system, are a further call to abandon the 'security' of the familiar Jewish rules and rituals, and to go out boldly into the risky new world of Christian discipleship, however much it may attract the scorn of the old régime.

FOR REFLECTION

In our very different situation, in what ways may we also be called to 'go out with Jesus', to settle for the uncomfortable way 'outside the camp'?

99 HEBREWS 13:15–19

FINAL INSTRUCTIONS

In these five verses, three further subjects are briefly introduced as the letter comes to its close: true sacrifices (vv. 15–16), respect for church leaders (v. 17), and prayer for the author of the letter (vv. 18–19).

True sacrifices

Verses 9–14 have focused on the distance which has now developed between the old sacrificial régime of the temple/tabernacle and the new Christian place of exile 'outside the camp'. These comments, together with the teaching of chapters 9 and 10 about the inadequacy of the Old Testament sacrifices and their eclipse now by the one perfect sacrifice of Christ, might suggest that a Christian church may now safely forget about 'sacrifice'. Not at all, says our author!

Animal sacrifices are now obsolete: Christ has offered the only atoning sacrifice which we can ever need. But there are other types of sacrifice for us to offer, not as means of obtaining God's grace and forgiveness, but in simple thanksgiving for the salvation we have received. The first is *praise*, the sort of 'spiritual sacrifice acceptable to God' which 1 Peter 2:5 calls for, and which is further defined there as 'proclaiming the mighty acts of him who called you out of darkness into his marvellous light' (1 Peter 2:9). For the lips that 'confess his name' cannot but speak of the saving acts which his very name denotes (especially in its Hebrew form Yahweh, the living God, and the name of Jesus, the Saviour).

But secondly there is also the sacrifice of *doing good*, without which any claim to Christian faith is a sham (James 2:14–26). 'Doing good' (v. 16) is very broad, but the author links it more specifically with 'sharing'. Here he uses a word (*koinonia*) which we often translate by 'fellowship' or 'communion', but which in the New Testament is very often used with a more directly financial and material sense, and that is the focus of the 'good works' called for in verse 16. The church which began its life in Jerusalem by practising 'Christian communism' (Acts 2:44–45; 4:32–37) remained throughout its early years a profoundly practical movement, concerned with meeting the material needs of its own members and of those outside it. It is an important question how far modern Christianity has remained faithful to its roots in this 'sacrificial' aspect of its service.

'Your leaders'

As well as the founders of the church whom they remembered with honour (13:7), there is a continuing recognized leadership, however they may have been described. Their responsibility is spiritual ('keeping watch over your souls') and given by God (to whom they will eventually 'give account'), and in fulfilling it they need the love and understanding of the rest of the church. An attitude of respectful support, shown by 'obeying' and 'submitting' (v. 17) rather than questioning and opposing, will enable them to fulfil their role of leadership with joy rather than with 'sighing' (a strong word, translated 'groan' in Romans 8:22, 23, 26). This is a heartfelt plea which would be echoed by many people in positions of church leadership today. Do you make your pastors 'groan'?

Pray for us

The writer of this letter also holds some position of leadership in relation to the church, though in his case from a distance for the time being. So, like Paul in many of his letters, he calls for his readers' prayers. He is conscious of a heavy responsibility, and apparently also of the danger of being misunderstood or misrepresented. While his own conscience is clear, he still feels vulnerable, and prayer support is needed.

More specifically, he wants them to pray that he will be able to return to them soon (v. 19). We know nothing of the circumstances which have detained him, but it is not surprising, in view of the deep concern for his church's spiritual health which he has displayed in this letter, that he is anxious to be back among them, rather than merely communicating from a distance.

FOR REFLECTION

These verses reveal interesting aspects of the life of an early Christian church and of the problems and responsibilities of leadership within it. How far do these insights find an echo in your own church and its leadership? Do you think that modern churches take sufficiently seriously the need for support and for prayer for their leaders?

100 HEBREWS 13:20–25

SIGNING OFF

Personal matters

The last four verses are similar to the personal conclusions of many New Testament letters. Verse 22 may provoke a wry smile as we wonder what a *long* 'word of exhortation' might have been like! If the Timothy of verse 23 is the same man who accompanied and assisted Paul in his travels and missionary work, and to whom the first two letters studied in this book were addressed, we know nothing of when or where he was imprisoned. Nor do we know the nature of his relationship to the author of this letter, but it seems that he, like Paul, found Timothy a congenial travelling companion and colleague in ministry.

The greeting mentions separately the leaders (see comments on 13:17) and the rest of the church ('all the saints'—'saints' being used in its normal New Testament sense of all the redeemed people of God, not just of a specially 'holy' sub-group). The separate mention of the leaders is no doubt designed to reinforce the appeal to the church members to give them due respect and support. Because we do not know the place and circumstances of writing, we cannot be sure why 'those from Italy' (v. 24) are associated with the author's greeting, but it is a reasonable guess that the church to which the letter was written was itself located in Italy (probably at Rome), and that these are expatriate members of the church who are now in touch with the author and wish to be remembered to their own people.

A rich concluding prayer

The real climax of the letter is in verses 20–21, with their resounding 'Amen', after which verses 22–25 are something of an anticlimax. These wonderful words, part prayer, part benediction, part doxology, have rightly come into frequent use as the conclusion to a Christian act of worship. They deserve careful unpacking: each of the following elements deserves a study in itself!

'The God of peace' is a title worth meditating on. 'Peace' is the positive antidote to disunity and to fear. In its Hebrew form, '*shalom*', it conveys an all-embracing sense of well-being. That is what life with God is all about.

This is the only mention of Jesus' resurrection in the whole letter. Elsewhere it is his exaltation to God's right hand that we have constantly been reminded of. But the two go together, and the victory of the resurrection is the basis of Jesus' unique authority.

'Great shepherd of the sheep' (a metaphor not used elsewhere in this letter, but common in the New Testament) sums up the saving and protecting work of Jesus which we have looked at from so many angles in this letter.

'The blood of the eternal covenant' reminds us of the whole argument of chapters 8—10: in Jesus' resurrection is the final demonstration that his one, perfect sacrifice has been accepted, that the way is now open to the blessings of the new covenant.

The prayer is that they may completely fulfil God's will by doing good. But this is not a matter of their own unaided moral strength, for it is God himself who gives his people the capacity to please him (compare the careful balance of responsibilities in Philippians 2:12–13). That is why a prayer like this (rather than simply an earnest moral exhortation) is both necessary and effective: in the end it is God who makes possible the doing of the will of God.

But, as this letter has insisted throughout, God's grace to his people is channelled uniquely 'through Jesus Christ', and it is a fitting and yet remarkably bold conclusion to this letter's portrayal of the divine authority of the Son that, in the final doxology, glory is ascribed not to God himself but rather to Jesus, who shares the Father's sovereignty and eternity.

PRAYER

God of peace, who brought back from the dead our Lord Jesus, the great shepherd of the sheep, by the blood of the eternal covenant, make us complete in everything good, so that we may do your will, working in us that which is pleasing in your sight, through Jesus Christ, to whom be the glory for ever and ever. Amen.

NOTES

NOTES

NOTES

NOTES

The People's Bible Commentary

Voucher Scheme

The People's Bible Commentary (PBC) provides a range of readable, accessible commentaries that will grow into a library covering the whole Bible.

To help you build your PBC library, we have a voucher scheme that works as follows: a voucher is printed on this page of each People's Bible Commentary volume (as above). These vouchers count towards free copies of other books in the series.

For every four purchases of PBC volumes you are entitled to a further volume FREE.

Please find the coupon for the PBC voucher scheme opposite.

All you need do:

- Cut out the vouchers from the PBCs you have purchased and attach them to the coupon.
- Complete your name and address details, and indicate your choice of free book from the list on page 224.
- Take the coupon to your local Christian bookshop who will exchange it for your free PBC book; or send the coupon straight to BRF who will send you your free book direct. Please allow 28 days for delivery.

Please note that PBC volumes provided under the voucher scheme are subject to availability. If your first choice is not available, you may be sent your second choice of book.